HARTMAN LOVELY 1250 3.00 PM

1307 - ARRIZ (GOOD NICK) SEVENE
CAST OFF

1308 - PURDEYS (20K) (CHECK CAST)
BIT MORE
BENT

Ferrets

1339 - AYAS (awful)

1326 - UGGIES (condition bad)

1504 - AYA (20 bore

1216 - °470 (15K.

AYA PREMIER (3200) ✓

.465 HOLLAND BOTH NEED
RESTOCKING

NEED REJOINTING

LATE ENTRY PURDEYS 18K
STRAIGHT ✓
1343 ➤

£18-22

Ferrets

D. BRIAN PLUMMER

Drawings by
DEREK E. HOMDEN

PERRY GREEN PRESS

British Library Cataloguing-in-Publication Data
A catalogue record for this book is available from
the British Library.

ISBN 1–902481–01–1

Printed in Great Britain by
The Lavenham Press Ltd., Lavenham, Suffolk

Contents

1

Polecats or Ferrets

If asked to describe the most exclusively British form of humour, an aspect of amusement neither found nor appreciated by any other nation on earth, I should be obliged to answer 'The riddle': a curious question, the answer to which relies on the use of either a homonym or an absurdity. For example, the riddle 'When is a door not a door?', is answered by the reply 'When it is a jar'. Likewise, 'Why did the chicken cross the road?', which merits the answer 'To get to the other side'. I confess I am jingoistically patriotic and hence feel almost ashamed to admit that, in common with the continentals, I too find the British obsession with riddles both irritating and pointless. Hence it is with some shame that my introduction to this book uses the self-same type of puzzle, the self-same sort of riddle I have just decried: 'When is a polecat not a polecat?', and the answer to such a riddle must be the most enigmatic of replies: 'When it is a ferret', It now behoves me to utilise the initial chapter of this book to explain the nature of such a riddle.

Despite the fact that most roads in the remote districts of Scotland and Wales are often littered with the cadavers of dark brown panda-faced mustelids, Dr Sleeman, *Stoats, Weasels, Polecats and Martens* (1989), describes the polecat as 'the most uncommon British member of the stoat-like creatures'. Indeed there is some evidence to suggest that the true British polecat Putorious Putorious is confined to certain areas around the Welsh town of Llandrindod Wells, a fairly isolated hilly region where ecologists first observed creatures they believed to be a pure form of the British or European polecat. They tagged and radio-tracked these animals in the 1970s, tracing their activities in rabbit warrens, badger sets, fox earths and the ever-present rat holes adjacent to barns and farmsteads.

So what are, or were, the polecat-coloured, polecat-shaped, polecat-smelling cadavers found on many country roads throughout Britain – and once again the answer must be 'ferrets' though whether these animals are feral ferrets, escapee ferrets, or even hybrid forms of ferrets and polecats can only be determined by a skilled biologist who has specialised in the study of mustelids (animals akin to, or related to, stoats).

So having introduced the reader to the enigma of the polecat and its domesticated relative, the ferret, it is perhaps expedient to investigate the origin of the domesticated ferret and, perhaps, by comparing the animal to its wild relative the European polecat, achieve a better under-standing of both species: though once again it should be pointed out that there is precious little evidence either palaeontological or historical to date the time when ferrets began to evolve from a certain species, or possibly certain species, of polecat.

It is virtually impossible to trace the history of any species of dom-esticate without referring to Zeuner's masterly *History of Domesticated Animals* (1963). Zeuner believes that the ferret is simply a domesticated form of the European or Asiatic polecat, though G.S. Miller, *Catalogue of the Mammals of Western Europe* (1912), states that the skull of the ferret almost exactly resembles that of the Steppe polecat, a slightly different, though very similar, creature to the European polecat.

Indeed Dr Sleeman believes that only by the examination of the skulls of road casualty polecat-coloured creatures can one determine as to whether the creature is a ferret or a wild European polecat, for there is a construction in the front of the cranium between the eyes of a ferret that is absent in a true wild polecat. Drabble, in his many books con-cerning field sports and the keeping of animals, believes that if a ferret is fed on the same diet as a wild polecat this difference in skull structure is not as obvious, but there is considerable evidence to suggest that Drabble is wrong. Once again the ease with which polecats hybridise with escapee ferrets, and produce fertile offspring from the unions, must produce progeny whose cranial structures would vary between that of the Asiatic polecat and the broader-headed European variety. However the situation is further complicated by the presence of pockets of feral ferrets throughout Britain.

Escapee ferrets have established themselves in the wild in a manner that Millais could never have envisaged. The species is now commonly seen – at least as commonly seen as a predator with the feeding habits of a mustelid is commonly seen – in the Isle of Man, districts in Cumbria, Lancashire and Yorkshire and in certain districts of the West of Scotland. On Mull, a district where the wild polecat had never been reported, polecat-ferret escapees began to establish themselves in 1933–34 and became a pest after the species had almost exterminated the abundant rabbit population of Mull and began preying on nesting gulls and domesticated poultry. Lever, *The Naturalised Animals of the British Isles* (1979), records that in 1922 a trapper (the name is used by Scots to describe a pest control officer) trapped twenty-two polecat-ferrets at Oskamull in 1944 and these ferrets differed little in habit or appearance from true wild polecats. Seton Gordon, *The Highland Year* (1944), mentions that when the rabbit plague of pre-myxomatosis days swept the island of Harris, reducing the grazing to such a state that many crofters were unable to wrest a living from the land, polecat-ferrets were released on the island to control the rabbit population. They were unable to curb the spread of the rabbit but were, in Seton Gordon's opinion, remarkably successful in exterminating the ptarmigan from this island.

Christopher Lever is, in fact, of the opinion that the true European polecat may well be extinct in Britain and reports of polecats usually turn out to be sightings of polecat-ferrets. It is interesting to note that the lustrous yellow undercoat of the wild polecat, so desired by German fitch farmers, is found in polecat-ferrets that have 'bred wild' for a season or so.

At the time of writing there are moves afoot, amongst conservationists and hunters alike, to reintroduce or increase the number of endangered or partially extinct species of animal that were once common in Britain. Dr Yapp's suggestion that wolves and wild boar should be reintroduced to the Highlands, brought a torrent of letters from outraged farmers who lived adjacent to the wilderness where Yapp suggested these introductions should take place. There have also been suggestions that both true polecats and martens should be reintroduced into certain areas of Britain in which the animals had once been reported; or to areas which seem ideally suited for the introduction of such species. However, at the risk of being accused of being anti-conservation in my approach to the future of the flora and fauna of Britain, it would be wise to study the history of the decline of a species before attempting to restock an area with that creature.

Contrary to popular opinion, or the notions of gamekeepers, neither polecats nor other mustelids have ever been particularly numerous in Great Britain. The very nature of the feeding habits of the species would ensure that the stoat-like creatures were naturally rare. Sleeman notes that an adult weasel would require point-eight ounces of meat per day to sustain its adult body weight, which would mean that a weasel would need to kill and devour at least one mouse per day feeding on all the bone, muscle tissue and viscera. Over a period of a single year a pair of weasels, rearing one or more litters of kittens, would therefore need to catch an enormous number of small rodents in order to exist. Hence while an area may boast a large number of mice and voles, weasels will be comparatively rare in such an area.

Polecats, which are larger animals than weasels, will need a considerably greater quantity of food in order to survive and procreate, and while it can be argued that a rabbit provides a greater quantity of food than a mouse (two-and-a-half to three-and-a-half pounds as opposed to one ounce) it can be counter-argued that rabbits are a relatively new species in Britain, and that prior to the introduction of the rabbit, the density of polecat numbers was governed by the availability of birds, small rodents and amphibians. Hence it seems unlikely that the polecat was ever particularly common in Great Britain and the sighting of a polecat would always have caused interest amongst countrymen. The notion that polecats were common near warrens was ludicrous, for the presence of a single pair of polecats near, or worse still within a rabbit warren, would have ensured the warren would have been somewhat less than profitable to maintain!

The somewhat rare polecat was destined to become the even more rare, and possibly extinct, polecat when a series of events irreversibly altered the ecology of Britain. After the British civil war improvements in musketry elevated Britain to the level of a world power, and such improvements were copied by the makers of sporting guns. Guns that were light, true, and accurate enough to shoot flying birds began to be manufactured and hence it became feasible for owners of large estates to make a considerable profit by rearing game birds and leasing the shooting rights on such estates to sportsmen.

Millais states that game bird rearing became so profitable that any bird with a curved bill and a predatory nature was ruthlessly persecuted, but no species was more ruthlessly slaughtered than were the mustelids. Stoats and weasels were trapped, shot, poisoned or killed by a dozen other barbarous means, but polecats, the traditional enemy of gallinaceous birds (la poule – a hen polecat – the hen cat) were the first species to bite the dust.

The incredible curiosity of the polecat was to be its undoing. I ask the reader to perform a simple experiment with a domesticated polecat – the ferret. Simply make a tunnel, by lifting a rug or carpet square, and place the ferret on the floor some distance from the tunnel. It is a racing certainty the ferret will be drawn as if by some irrestible magnet to explore the tunnel made by the fold of the rug. Such curiosity was to be the downfall of the wild polecat which became one of the easiest animals for the keeper to catch. A tunnel trap, set with a gin trap within, slew great numbers of stoats, weasels, polecats and martens, for traps, which would have alerted the most unwary of rats to the dangers within them, became sources of fascination for the curious mustelids.

What created even greater enmity towards the genus was the

phenomena known to modern behaviourists as 'surplus killing', an action never quite understood by our more anthropomorphic ancestors who branded the genus as blood-maddened killers, soulless demons, intent on the destruction of any small, and apparently defenceless, creature. The mustelids, the most fascinating of small mammals, all took on an unwholesome image because of their tendency to indulge in spates of surplus killing.

When a small or medium sized mustelid finds a way into a poultry pen, or a game rearing pen, where the birds are confined or unable to escape, the animal may kill all the birds but eat only a very small quantity of the birds it has killed. This spate of killing is not due to some psychopathic vicious streak in the animal, but is due to the stoat, weasel, polecat or marten achieving what behaviourists refer to as 'a super-stimulus of available prey' – something that would never happen under natural conditions, for if it did the prey species would be removed from the area in which it resided and the predator would literally starve itself into extinction. Once a mustelid, living in natural conditions, has killed enough prey to satisfy its desire to eat, it refrains from further killing until it is hungry again. There are records of stoats having killed young rats, eating their victim while young rats from the same litter emerge to feed a dozen or so yards from the stoat, behaving as if they were aware that the stoat, having eaten its fill, will, at least for the time being, pose no further threat to the rats. The feasts of gore described by Victorian gamekeepers, seldom occurred, except, that is, in the game rearing pens, for a delicate ecological balance must exist between the prey and the predator if both species are to continue to survive.

Wild polecats eat a great variety of mammalian, avian, amphibian and reptilian prey. Rabbits, young rats (seldom old or strong healthy rats one should add), mice and voles are supplemented with a diet of birds (cripples, ground nesting and nesting birds) amphibians and reptiles – and polecats are reputedly able to slay adders in the manner that mongooses kill cobras and kraits. The strange story of the polecat's larder of leucotomised frogs, bitten through the brains, paralysed but still alive, food on the hoof for the polecat's off-days, is questioned by many. Hubbard states that the tale is well authenticated, but Sleeman believes that this story is yet another example of the legends of the alleged atrocities perpetrated by various mustelids but cannot be substantiated by fact.

Before leaving the subject of the diet of the wild European polecat, it must be expedient to discuss the subject of sexual dimorphism. Male mustelids are always much larger than females of the same species. Since the early 1900s ecologists have believed that sexual dimorphism is an adaptation which has developed to allow both male and female mustelids to co-exist in the same area without competing for the same prey species. In short, males are capable of catching and killing stronger, more powerful prey animals than the smaller females. For instance a female polecat is capable of venturing into rat holes and killing and eating young grey rats – though the male, by its very size, is incapable of catching young rats by this method. However, recent research into sexual dimorphism has produced evidence that does not support the notion that the variation in size between the sexes is simply an adaptation that allows both male and female mustelids to hunt the same area.

The Erlinge-Moors hypothesis arrived at independently by S. Erlinge in 1972 and P.J. Moors in 1983 suggests that female mustelids are considerably smaller than the males of the same species in order to conserve their energy while raising litters of kittens – though the small size does allow the female to enter the lairs of small rodents and lagomorphs. Many ecologists are not prepared to accept the Erlinge-Moors hypothesis it should be added.

The hypothesis has its short-comings, particularly if it is examined in the light of the lifestyle of the polecat. Polecats mate and produce young in early summer, a time when there is an abundance of nesting birds and small immature rodents – easy pickings for a polecat – so seemingly May would be the ideal time for most British woodland and moorland predators to produce their young. However, May is also the time when polecats, both male and female, start to lose their coats and the moult involves a tremendous loss of energy, for the animal must regain its new coat, an action that utilises a great deal of proteinous material particularly as the moult coincides with the time when jill polecats are hard pressed to find enough prey to feed a growing litter. Seemingly polecat metabolism is not entirely geared to energy conservation.

It would also be a mistake to assume that all predatory species enjoy the same type of sexual dimorphism. Accipitrids such as sparrowhawks produce young at roughly the same time as do polecats, stoats and weasels and for the self-same reason – an abundance of nesting birds and immature easily-caught rodents. Here, however, the female sparrowhawk can often be twice as large as the thrush-sized musket or male sparrowhawk.

Before leaving the subject of the sexual differences between male and female mustelids, it is perhaps expedient to mention the bizarre sexual habits of mustelids in general and the European polecat in particular, and few genuses indulge in such weird and quite unique sexual behaviour as do the mustelids. Stoats, long the epitome of rampant sexuality in Anglo-Saxon folklore, indulge in the most amazing socio-sexual behaviour. Adult male stoats not only sire a litter of young stoats, but mount and fertilise the female kit stoats before the kits have opened their eyes and are ready to leave the nest – before the kits are thirty-five days old in fact. Sleeman, an authority on the Irish stoat suggests that this incredible sexual behaviour is probably due to the fact that the stoat is one of the most short-lived of mustelids and this factor alone prevents intensive inbreeding amongst the species – 'the male that has mated with the mother the previous summer is very often replaced by another the following summer' – a somewhat illogical explanation for the incestuous behaviour of adult male stoats.

Male polecats are perhaps not as incestuous in their mating habits, but indulge in the same furious mating techniques. Mating stimulates ovulation, hence copulation can last for an hour or more with much chattering while the male seizes the back of the female's neck, macerates the nape of the neck with its teeth and produces a marked erythema of the skin of the female's neck during the mating process. Female ferrets, domesticated polecats confined too closely with a particularly vigorous male, often suffer considerable damage from the amorous attentions of the hob. In the wild, polecats occupy a large territory and are hence able to escape the attention of a highly sexed male. Ordinarily mating takes place within the male's territory and a male polecat may cover a few but seldom several females, for males have a fairly fixed territory and few areas are so heavily stocked with rodents, small birds and lagomorphs as to support a very large polecat population.

Tiny kits or kittens are born in dens, in rocks or rabbit holes and sometimes, though more rarely, derelict rat burrows. Kittens are born blind and naked and remain blind for some thirty-five days and Sleeman notes that, from this age onwards, male polecats grow more quickly than females – sexual dimorphism does in fact start to occur from the fifth week of birth onwards. This long period of 'blindness' is said to be beneficial to the furtherance of the species for mustelids are extremely precocious and as soon as their eyes are open tend to explore regions adjacent to the nesting site. It seems that these polecats remain blind until they have acquired some discretion (an anthropomorphic expression perhaps) or sense enough to evade or warn off possible predators. It is also beneficial to the jill or doe polecat to be able to find her young still in the nest when she returns to the den with her kills. Ferrets become decidedly disturbed if a kit leaves the nest prematurely, either by crawling towards the opening of the lair or by adhering to a female's teat and being pulled from the nest. Jills and sometimes even hobs (if the hob is left with kindling females) will rush out and seize a wayward kit and restore it to the nest. If two or more jill ferrets are allowed to kindle in the same nest (this situation would never, or hardly ever, occur in the wild as polecats are solitary creatures and females seldom nest close together and never share a communal nest, will pull each other back to the communal nest at feeding time). There is scant evidence to suggest that wild female nursing polecats finding a nest of polecat kits belonging to another nursing jill will steal and adopt the kits rather than cannabalise the litter. In 1987 a part-time keeper, Paul Richards, wrote to me to state that he had observed what he believed to be a wild polecat jill dart in and out of a den carrying with her polecat kittens which she deposited in another den. This behaviour might be explained by the fact that polecat jills will often move their litters between dens, though ferrets, when bred in communes, will often filch each others' litters to adopt rather than eat them. Cannibalism, of course, does occur if kits are repeatedly taken to and from nests by two or more jills who become distressed by the theft of their kittens. Communal ferret breeding schemes, extremely popular at the time of writing, are, despite the ease by which ferret kits are reared in these conditions, extremely unnatural and are certain to result in higher mortality rates than if the jills were allowed to kindle in separate cages. The squealing of kittens is apparently just as distressing to a female polecat as to a female ferret and hence it is not unlikely that Richards did observe a jill stealing and adopting another polecat jill's litter.

The play of ferrets and wild polecats (both kittens and adults alike) is both fascinating and enigmatic. Groos *The Play of Animals and the Play of Man* describes play as preparatory for real-life situations. Polecat play is exaggerated with snake-like jerky movements that resemble the antics of a cartoon animal, rather than that of a real life creature, but the element of restraint is evident in each and every play pattern. If either animal sustains the slightest hurt or the merest injury during the game, play stops immediately and the animal that has engendered this unintentional hurt is obviously disturbed. Both kits and adults alike indulge in wrestling games and kick vigorously, but not vigorously enough to injure throughout the 'battle'. Spencer defines the difference between play and reality as simply that play involves the element of restraint and never is this element of restraint more obvious than in the play patterns of ferocious predators.

Sleeman remarks on that peculiar phenomenom the adoption of the play face: an expression manifested by both fierce predators and also primates. The play face expression is characterised by the open relaxed mouth – and ferrets which manifest this expression will seldom bite in earnest if handled. Polecats and ferrets indulge in wild chases during these play sessions and encourage a playmate to follow them and continue with the game by adopting the 'play face' expression. There is a school of thought that suggests this peculiar patterning of the face of the typical European polecat not only gives an indication to the potential predator that the polecat is unpleasant to eat – skunks display similar contrasting markings to deter potential predators – but allows the animal to communicate a greater number of moods and messages to members of its own species. It is interesting to note the majority of German guard dog breeds – German Shepherd dogs, Dobermanns, Rottweilers – are not only black-and-tan or black-and-brown but display facial patterns that tell a trainer or another dog much of the moods of the animal. Lowry remarks that police dog or guard dog trainers are hesitant to train white GSDs, not merely because white dogs seldom inspire the same fear in would-be aggressors but because the absence of distinct facial markings on the face of white or cream GSDs denies the animal its complete potential of facial expressions in order to indicate its moods. The markings on the face of a black-and-tan dog undergo an apparent transformation as a prelude to the animal attacking an adversary.

The methods adopted by polecats to kill suitable prey seldom vary. Mice and grey rats are usually killed by a random bite and the pressure of the polecats jaws extinguishes life from the prey. Rats, or rather large powerful rats, are usually avoided by stoats, weasels and wild polecats simply because the rat's powers of retaliation are vastly underrated by casual observers. Lorenz summarises the situation nicely and states that a predator must be able to slay its prey with the prey inflicting only the minimum damage to its attacker – a lion slightly injured each and every time it slays a gemsbok for instance would not survive long enough to perpetuate its species. Rats, or once again adult powerful healthy rats, are usually avoided by mustelids up to the size of a marten simply because rats retaliate with great ferocity when attacked – though there is some, albeit slight, evidence that young mustelids are not instinctively afraid or wary of adult rats but soon learn the error of their ways and ever after avoid conflict with a dangerous adversary such as a rat. Young greys, rats not old enough to breed, are usually dispatched, and dispatched fairly quickly by a bite to the rear of the head or an incision made near the atlas or axis vertebra.

Rabbits are dispatched by a slightly different technique: they are seldom killed in open country for a polecat is usually unable to outpace and kill a healthy fleeing rabbit. Rabbits slain by polecats are usually bottled up in a stop (a blind-ended tube) under the warren and slain by a bite to the base of the skull or through the eyes of the rabbit. Rabbits which struggle or kick violently will apparently deter the attacks of all but the most persistent polecat and even the larger male polecats will sometimes back down if kicked viciously by a bottled-up rabbit. Likewise there are well-authenticated tales of stoats and weasels slain by sitting game birds – killed by a particularly vicious peck or a sharp and hurting blow from the edges of the wings of these birds.

It is often stated that both polecats and ferrets are detered from attacking by the inertia manifested by a rabbit infected with myxomatosis and are said to nose and nudge the rabbit in an attempt to make the rabbit show some sign of life. No doubt all mustelids have found the untypical behaviour of infected rabbits slightly puzzling, but a hungry polecat or a wild jill hunting to feed a hungry litter of kits would soon overcome her aversion to killing an infected rabbit. Certainly the remains of cadavers of infected conies have been found at, or near, the lairs of polecat kittens.

Polecats, particularly polecat jills nursing litters of kittens, are not averse to feeding on carrion – an action that frequently brings about the downfall of the animal. Road casualty animals, birds and reptiles, are not infrequent along certain stretches of country roads and polecats attempting to feed on these macerated cadavers often become road casualties themselves. Normally mustelids are reluctant to feed on related species but in this respect polecats display more catholic tastes. Road casualty badger carcasses are often used as sources of food by male and female polecats alike and ferrets certainly find badger meat acceptable. Stoats and weasels cadavers, and those of other ferrets and polecats, are disdained by both polecats and ferrets even when other food is scarce, but kittens or the remains of kittens are sometimes found in the breeding dens of polecat jills. Whether these kittens are killed by polecats has been questioned by some naturalists, for cats are incredibly aggressive if a hostile intruder approaches a lair where kittens are residing. However, it is equally true to state that some queens are remiss about rearing their litters and often abandon their first litters of kittens for no apparent reason. Whether polecats will kill the progeny of feral cats or simply devour dead kittens is debatable but unimportant. Sufficient to say, that courageous as British mustelids are prone to be, they are over-matched by an adult queen cat, though there are well-authenticated tales of stoat packs (a female stoat and her family of nearly mature kittens) attacking cats, dogs and even people.

Both polecats and ferrets seek out and eat the eggs of ground nesting birds with great enthusiasm. The behaviour of both polecats and stoats when dealing with hen's eggs has interested many naturalists. The search to find a way into the egg to devour the contents often degenerates into a game, with the animals pawing and batting the egg to and fro until the egg shell breaks or cracks. Polecats that are not so famished as to furiously seek out food, will waste no opportunity to indulge in a game of any sort even with the cadaver of an animal they have just found or recently killed.

Thus the natural history of the polecat: the ancestor of the domesticated ferret, or if Lever is correct that the British polecat is long extinct perhaps the animals studied by modern naturalists are simply feral ferrets, the skulls of which have adapted to a more natural lifestyle and a purely carnivorous diet (Drabble). The enigma of the polecat becomes even more baffling when one investigates the origin of the domesticated form of the polecat – the ferret.

2

From Polecat to Ferret

In common with Sleeman, Zeuner *History of Domesticated Animals* is of the opinion that the ferret is not simply a domesticated form of the European polecat, but a descendant of the slightly narrower-skulled steppe polecat Putorious Eversmanii. Haagerdoorn, the Dutch geneticist, is of the opinion that the ferret may well be polyphyletic: derived from more than one species namely the steppe polecat and the closely related, but slightly different, European polecat. Once again it should be pointed out that Haagerdoorn's theory is scarcely supported by factual evidence for he states that the European polecat, the fitch, is literally untameable. This is simply not true, for while wild polecats caught as adults fail to adjust to captivity and often remain savage and unhandleable until their demise, young polecat kits taken from the nest before their eyes open become as tame, or nearly as tame, as domesticated ferrets. It would require only a brief spell of domestication and a fairly rigorous selection of suitable handleable animals to produce serviceable 'ferrets' from the progeny of wild-bred European 'polecats'.

It has been argued that, because the domesticated ferret more closely resembles the steppe polecat than the European polecat, the ferret was first domesticated in the east and imported into Europe. Conversely, it has been suggested that because the sole purpose of domesticating polecats was to reduce the rabbit population of certain areas, the polecat must have been domesticated in certain lands adjacent to the Mediterranean – the homeland of the rabbit.

Aristotle, vague and scarcely accurate as only Aristotle is allowed to be, describes a type of polecat that was 'very mild and tame', but declines to mention as to the purpose for which the animal was used, and furthermore in the fourth century before Christ it seems unlikely that Aristotle or his fellow home-dwelling Greeks would have ever seen or heard of the rabbit which was at that time still confined to certain regions of the Iberian peninsula. Yet Aristophanes, writing a century earlier than

Aristotle, refers to a similar animal kept by the Boeotians (ictis) though Thomson *History of the Ferret* (1951) suggests that both Aristotle's and Aristophane's ictis might refer to another mustelid, perhaps a marten or more likely still a mongoose. Zeuner believes that the 'ictis' of Aristotle and Aristophanes may well have been a ferret or a partly domesticated polecat, for whereas the rabbit had not made its appearance in Greece at this time, ferrets might well have been kept to control certain rodents. Zeuner, however, is obviously not conversant with the ways of ferrets or polecats. No ferret is fast enough to catch free-moving mice, nor small enough to creep into the lairs of these tiny rodents and destroy them, and scarcely able to climb well enough to be a serious threat to the more arboreal black rat. Furthermore the larger brown rat had not yet made its appearance in Europe or if it had had never become an established species before the eighteenth century. I believe the 'ictis' of Aristotle or Aristophanes to be a domesticated Egyptian or Asiatic mongoose: a more quicksilver creature capable of catching small rodents in and around houses and scarcely as likely to wander as would be a ferret or polecat.

Reference is often made to the mention of the ferret in the James Edition of the *Holy Bible* (Leviticus 11 v.30) in the dietary code of the Hebrews, for the ferret was one of the creatures the Hebrews were forbidden to eat. However, recent research into the animals mentioned in the Old Testament has caused theological scholars to think again about the translation they have afforded certain creatures mentioned there. The unicorn (re'em), mentioned some seven times in the Old Testament, has now been translated as rhinocerus, and the ferret of Leviticus has now been transmuted to land-lizard by modern translators.

Likewise Strabo's reference to ferrets must be questioned. Strabo, 58 BC–AD 24 was a widely travelled Roman writer and historian who wrote up his travels in some seventeen books known collectively as *Geographia*. In one of his accounts of his journeys he mentions a plague of rabbits that had caused such distress to the natives of the Balearic Islands that the population asked to either, be re-homed on a rabbit-free island, or that Augustus send a legion of soldiers to clear the island of its problem conies. Strabo records that the Emperor chose to send troops with muzzled Lybian ferrets to rid the island of its rabbits. Whether Strabo's Lybian ferrets were a type of Egyptian mongoose has long been debated for the polecat is absent in the fauna of Africa. Zeuner suggests that Lybian ferrets may well be a breed rarity or simply a misnomer in the same way as Belgian Hares (a variety of domesticated rabbit) is neither a hare nor from Belgium. The 'ferret' mentioned by Pliny, often styled the father of modern naturalists, in his book *Naturalis Historia* has all the qualities of a mongoose rather than those of a domesticated polecat.

When the ferret was brought to Britain has never been established, though there would have been little work for the creature before rabbits were introduced and kept within walled or fenced enclosures known as warrens. Rabbits were kept within these enclosures and, unlike hares, bred freely in these conditions. Varro, said to be the founder of commercial rabbit breeding, was said to be the first to realise the commercial potential of keeping rabbits within these enclosures which were often raised with piles of sticks, brushwood and stones to afford adequate drainage, which was so essential for a Mediterranean-type creature such as the rabbit to breed and grow. I have dealt with the subject of the upkeep of these warrens more fully in my book *In Pursuit of Coney* so repetition would not be expedient. Sufficient to say that when rabbits were required for the table a warrener (one responsible for the upkeep of these commercial warrens) would insert a ferret into the burrows and net the bolting rabbits. It is interesting to note that about AD 600 (a time when commercial warrens were already well-established on the continent if not in Britain) one Isidore of Seville describes an animal used in rabbit hunting (the rabbit was indigenous to the Iberian Peninsula and had been observed feeding on the eastern shores of Spain by the Phoenicians in 1100 BC. In fact the Phoenicians likened the rabbit to the hyrax, the coney of Biblical times, and named the peninsula *i shephanim* – the coast of the coney/hyrax/rabbit which later became latinised to Hispania (Spain and Portugal). Isidore of Seville called the small animal used to bolt rabbits to the nets 'furo' probably from the Latin *a thief* and it seems likely, but not entirely certain, the word ferret came from this root – though why one should associate the ways of a polecat or ferret with those of a thief is questionable, and frankly I feel the word ferret may well be derived from a somewhat different, though possibly long forgotten, root.

For some reason the majority of books concerned with ferrets and ferreting seem to assume that the ferrets first imported to Britain were white in colour: albinistic forms of the polecat identical to the 'whites' advertised today. In all probability the original ferrets brought to Britain by Norman or Angevin warreners would have been little different in colour, shape or size to the steppe polecat. It has always been assumed that the polecat-coloured ferrets seen today are the result of mating these early imported white ferrets to European polecats – and it is assumed that these dark-coloured ferrets are the result of escapee white jills coupling with wild polecat males. This is quite absurd. White ferrets are simply albinistic sports found in litters of dark polecat-coloured ferrets, and the white strains bred by simply breeding from these white sports because these white ferrets were considered to be more unusual, more attractive or more conspicuous than their polecat-coloured siblings.

Yet while it is patently obvious to zoologists of the calibre of Zeuner and Sleeman that the ferret is simply a domesticated form of the polecat with which the ferret will both mate and produce fertile hybrids, many Victorian writers disputed this notion. Nicholas Everitt believed the ferret was, in fact, an entirely separate species, quite distinct from the European polecat and desperately reaching for a translation of Strabo's *Geographica* states the species originated in Africa – a continent that boasts no variety of wild polecat.

Harting, more famous for his quote 'one thing is certain the rabbit will always be with us' than for his literary skills, or ability to research a subject meticulously, remarks that 'The better opinion is that the ferret is merely a domesticated variety of polecat with which it is frequently crossed for the purpose of improving the breed'.

Marchington in his book *Pugs and Drummers* states that he would, were it not for scientific evidence to the contrary, prefer to believe that the ferret was a type of stoat grown larger, rather than a type of polecat bred smaller 'for the natural consequences of domestication of a creature is for it to grow larger not smaller' – there are countless examples from geese to rabbits to prove the point. How Marchington arrives at such a conclusion is bewildering. Zeuner states that one of the second stages of domestication of an animal 'involves subjugating large numbers of the species and making these individuals wholly dependant on the social medium of man'. The outcome of this process was a stock with distinct characters of domestication – such as different colours and reduction of size – and in this respect the ferret would seem to be an excellent example of how social contact with man had brought about a predict-able metamorphosis from the wild polecat. The fact that the ferret is virtually identical to the wild polecat, from which it most certainly evolved, engaging in the same play patterns, the same mating and court-ship rituals, and the same gestation period seems to be overlooked by most Victorian naturalists many of whom simply sought to find the extraordinary in the commonplace.

On the subject of introducing wild polecat blood to revitalise and improve the working qualities of the ferret, the notion has experienced a revival in recent years as the spate of advertisements for wild polecat-X-ferret kits attests. These litters all seem to share a common origin: a conception as 'mystical' as that of a Celtic superhero perhaps. Usually the tale emerges that a jill ferret has gone missing during a ferreting trip late in the season, at a time when the jill was either near or in season. Later the lost jill (usually a white jill incidentally) is recovered and found to be in kindle. It is assumed that the sire of the litter, all or most of which were dark fitch-coloured, was a wild polecat hob, and hence the litters are usually advertised as wild polecat-X-ferret hybrids though both the origin of this litter and the word hybrid are suspect to say the least!

I am frequently asked about the authenticity of these litters via my weekly column in *Shooting News* and other magazines, but the subject remains an enigma. Firstly, if Lever is correct the wild polecat became extinct, or extremely rare, in Britain (so rare as for it to be highly unlikely for an amorous male polecat to encounter and serve an in-season jill ferret) at the turn of the twentieth century. However, Lever mentions that large areas of Britain host a huge feral ferret population and thus the sire of the litters just described allegedly (wild polecat-X-ferret) is quite likely to be a feral ferret hob, polecat in colour perhaps, but a ferret and not a wild polecat.

Of the two litters of allegedly polecat-X-ferret shown to me during my trip South in 1987 one litter was composed of eight kittens, six of which were a dark lustrous fitch colour and two were white. It would therefore seem likely that the hob that had covered this white jill ferret was a dark polecat-coloured ferret which carried white genes. However, it is not entirely improbable, though it is highly unlikely, that certain genuine wild polecat hobs would carry the genes that create albinism and thus, mated to an albino jill ferret, would produce some albino kittens. After all, white ferrets certainly appeared as sports in normal polecat-coloured litters, and breeders intrigued with the rarity value of these creatures continued to breed from these sports and produced albino strains of ferret (albinism is recessive so an albino sport mated to an albino-coloured mate would produce all white kits). However, it must be stressed that it is highly unlikely that any true wild polecat hob (sans domesticated ferret blood) would both carry the genes for albinism and meet up with, and cover, a stray albino-coloured jill ferret or a polecat-coloured jill that carried the genes for albinism.

However, let us assume that, by the merest chance, a true wild polecat, pure bred and completely free of ferret blood should meet up with, and mate, a jill ferret, it is extremely questionable as to whether the infusion of wild polecat blood would improve a strain of working ferret. This 'revert to the wild to renew long lost vigour' notion dates to the early 1950s when Haagerdoorn published his two controversial, and frankly highly inaccurate books, *Animal Breeding* and *Plant Breeding*: two books that advanced the premise that when man domesticated certain

17

varieties of plant and animal the domesticates lost much of their immunity to disease (wild potatoes are supposedly more immune to blight than most varieties of cultivated potato) and much of the natural vigour acquired over several million years of Darwinian natural selection. However, having explained Haagerdoorn's hypothesis and hypothesis it seems likely to remain, let us return to the possible merits conferred by adding a dash of genuine wild polecat blood to a strain of working ferret.

It might be assumed that this dash of alien blood might confer hybrid vigour to the progeny. However this hybrid vigour may equally readily be introduced by mating a jill ferret to a totally unrelated hob, particularly if both hob and jill were bred from inbred (but unrelated) strains of ferret, for a polecat is simply the wild ancestor of the domesticated ferret – despite the misgivings and theories of Everitt and, perhaps, Marchington.

Domestication may have taken the edge off ferrets as Haagerdoorn believes, but generations of domestication, selection and breeding from only the most gentle and handleable ferrets has certainly produced a type of ferret that is not only easier to handle but considerably easier to work. True polecats bred from wild stock, which are naturally more suspicious than their domesticated cousins would be singularly out of place in a ferreting party where their nervous disposition would ensure they skulked, peeping from holes, fearful of leaving the sanctuary of the lair and willing to nip rather than submit to being handled – hardly qualities one would require in a strain of working ferret.

It can, however, be argued that wild polecat blood would produce a faster, more agile, harder biting type of hybrid kitten (and once more the word hybrid should be suspect). However it must be asked if the ferreter requires an animal that has these qualites. Does a rabbit hunter want a hyperactive, furiously fast, hard biting ferret that not only finds its rabbit quickly and efficiently, but dispatches that rabbit with the alacrity of a wild polecat, and begins to feed on the carcass in the manner of its wild ancestor. Most ferrets are quite fast enough to satisfy the most impatient of ferreters, and it is easier to extract a bolted rabbit from purse nets rather than dig to a ferret that is lying up on its kill – despite the ease with which modern ferret locators direct the ferreter to the proximity of a kill, and the ferret that is eating the rabbit carcass.

It has been argued that polecat blood may enable the kittens from such a union to be superlative ratting ferrets with a willingness to attack doe rats (bucks are usually only too keen to bolt to a ferret) that exceeds that of an ordinary jill ferret. Once again these theories fail to hold water. If Lorenz is correct, and it appears that he is, few wild animals are prepared to attack prey which will engender the predator considerable hurt – and there is ample evidence to suggest that wild stoats, weasels and polecats are reluctant to attack any adult doe rat that has either gathered bedding to prepare for a litter (at this time doe rats are exceedingly fierce), or is protecting a litter of young naked kits. In this respect many of the strains of ferret, particularly the greyhound strains, long-bodied slender ferrets specifically bred for ratting were considerably more game (or perhaps foolhardy is a more appropriate word) than wild polecats.

Thus there seems little advantage in introducing wild polecat blood into a strain of working ferret, particularly if that strain is tractable, easily handled and free from the nervousness that makes any ferret a nuisance to own. Litters born to jills that have escaped, or been lost during a hunting foray, and have coupled with fathers of questionable lineage should be regarded as ferrets and not polecat/ferret hybrids.

In closing, the weasel/ferret hybrids advertised by a breeder near Box Hill, Surrey, that caused considerable interest in 1980 when the breeder advertised the litter in the pages of the sporting papers were simply small, undersized ferrets of the sort it now seems fashionable and fairly profitable to breed. It is virtually impossible to hybridise any of the mustelids, and hence tales of stoat-X-ferret, weasel-X-ferret and mink-X-ferret should be treated with some reserve. True in these days when hybrid predatory birds are readily and easily produced by artificial insemination – gyr falcons-X-sakers, gyr peregrines, perlins (merlins-X-peregrines) and other species hybrids it would seem probable that man may well be able to breed the most amazing and unlikely chimaeras by dint of artificial insemination. It is sufficient to say that to date, so complex are the reproduction processes of mustelids and so little is known of the reproductive capacities of these creatures that no scientifically authenticated hybrids have been produced.

Thus the polecat, its kith and kin, and its domesticated form, the common ferret. Now it is expedient to explore the keeping and use of ferrets.

3

Hobs, Jills, Size and Colour

Despite the fact that the ferret would have been almost unknown in Britain before the Norman Conquest, the sexes of ferrets have decidedly Anglo-Saxon names; for the males are referred to as hobs (or dogs) and the females jills (or bitches). The sexual dimorphism that characterises polecats dictates the males are decidedly larger and more powerful than the females, though, generally speaking, the domesticated ferret is considerably smaller than its wild ancestor. Marchington, *Pugs and Drummers*, quotes the average weight of the polecat to be two and three-quarter pounds in the case of the hob and one and three-quarter pounds in the case of the female: well in excess of the weight of the ferret. Lever, *The Naturalised Animals of the British Isles*, quotes identical weights for feral polecat ferrets. McKay, *The Ferret and Ferreting Handbook*, states the average weight of the ferret as between fourteen ounces in the case of the jill and four pounds the weight of a large, indeed a very large, hob.

At the time of writing there is a tendency for hunters, and ferret keepers alike, to favour very small animals – finger-sized jill ferrets are not only regularly produced but find a ready market. Conversely, large hobs are extremely difficult to sell and ferret breeders often find it very difficult to sell hobs of any size. Hence many males are destroyed at birth by ferret keepers who are aware they may not be able to sell their wares. Yet, the destruction of hob kittens and the breeding of very tiny ferrets is a short-sighted policy and shows that breeders often have little knowledge of the furious tumult that takes place below ground when a ferret encounters a rabbit.

It has been argued that a hob, particularly a large and powerful hob, will attack a rabbit, kill it all too easily, or prevent the rabbit from bolting, and since the invention of ferret locators, which enable the ferreter to find and dig to his ferret quickly and efficiently, ferrets that catch, hold or kill their quarry are prized by some ferreters. Yet there is little conclusive evidence to suggest that hobs are more efficient at killing bottled up rabbits than are jills. When a rabbit seeks the sanctuary of the stop (a blind ended tunnel in an established warren sometimes used by pregnant does to nest and rear a litter) it pushes its head into the blind end of the stop and pushes its haunches towards its foe hunching its rump to prevent the ferret or stoat climbing over the rabbits haunches to insert the fatal head bite. A large hob will attempt to pull the rabbit from the stop in order to slay it, but it requires a hefty tug from a human hand to pull the rabbit from such a stop. The ferret will now attempt to scratch at the rabbit's rump to encourage it to move, and may denude the rump of hair by its efforts, but should the rabbit remain resolute and refrain from moving, there is a distinct possibility even the largest hob will tire of its efforts and leave the rather bedraggled, bare-rumped rabbit to live to fight another day.

A tiny jill may well emulate the actions of the hob, but will be more successful at clambering over the back of the rabbit and inserting a fatal bite. In doing so the smallest jill might succeed at clambering over the rabbit, kill the rabbit, and be trapped or prevented from coming to the surface by the carcass of the rabbit that, in death, may relax its muscles alter its shape and trap the ferret until the ferret can eat its way out of its 'prison', or in exceptional cases be suffocated by the rabbit's carcass cutting off the ferret's air supply. Some jills become very efficient at killing rabbits in stops and unless such jills are fitted with locator collars can become great nuisances that are soon lost if the ferreter decides to work deep, or established, burrows.

Finger-sized jills, no matter how courageous they may be – and some are suicidally courageous – often suffer badly during a ferreting foray, even when the quarry hunted is the rabbit. Ferreters often underestimate the frenzied activity taking place below ground when a ferret attempts to bolt (it seems unlike any ferret wishes to bolt a rabbit so that it will be entrapped in the nets) or endeavours to kill the rabbit. Few rabbits accept their fate without a desperate struggle when a ferret attacks a coney below ground. Many ferreters interpret the furious bumping, that often precedes the bolting of a rabbit, with a stamping sound often used by alpha-bucks and does to alert the rest of the occupants of the burrow to possible danger. In point of fact there is considerable evidence to suggest that the sound of bumping emanates from a desperate struggle between the rabbit and the ferret attacking it. It is a mistake to believe the tales of petrified rabbits, frozen to immobility, awaiting inevitable death with the stoicism of a Zeno. Rabbits will often fight mustelids with great fury when driven to a state of desperation by imminent death. Some years ago, long before I was wise enough or prosperous enough to speculate in a locator and collar contraption, the sound of a furious struggle some metres below the surface of the soil alerted Penguin – a long-dead lurcher bitch – to the presence of a ferret attacking a rabbit. Penguin marked the sound of the tumult and I dug to the cacophanous bumping. A mere spit down I broke through to a rabbit facing a small jill ferret that the two-and-a-half pound doe was clearly in the process of outmatching. At the end of many successful rabbiting seasons in Caithness my ferrets have developed a slightly moth-eaten, slightly below par, appearance and a sensitivity to touch that indicates that the season has been not only hectic but a decidedly bruising one. Lest the reader advances the theory that my observations are inaccurate, and that Lorenz states that a predator is unlikely to attack any prey animal that will cause it anything but the slightest of hurts, it should be mentioned that whereas a wild polecat is unlikely to kill two rabbits a week throughout the year, a ferret might be required to attack, and attempt to bolt or kill, as many as fifty rabbits in a single day's ferreting. Tiny jills suffer quite badly from tussles with rabbits. Frankly, if the ferreter intends to participate in a hectic season of rabbiting, working a ferret as much as four days a week in country with a strong stock of healthy rabbits, he would be wise to chose a large powerful jill or a medium-sized hob rather than one of the tiny mites that seem to be so popular at the time of writing.

Such ferrets fare very badly if ratted regularly for, despite the fact that the majority of rats bolt rather than taking the fight to the ferrets – and many ratting ferrets often emerge totally unscathed after bolting an entire warren of rats – a doe (always the shaitan of ferrets) that decides to fight, rather than run, will make red ruin of any of the very popular tiny ferrets being bred today. I shall however deal more fully with the subject of ratting later in the book.

One reason for the production of these tiny ferrets becomes obvious when one considers the enormous pet market for ferrets in Britain and more so in America where 'de-scented' ferrets are popular flat pets. It is certainly easier for the ferret breeder to dispose of a litter of very tiny ferrets than it would be for him to sell a litter of normal-sized kits.

Yet it is fair to state that hobs are not nearly as versatile as jills, for the work of male ferrets must be exclusively to bolt rabbits, or to fulfil any of the other functions a ferret must perform while rabbiting (these will be explained in detail later in this book). A jill, by dint of her smaller size, can be used to work rat; for few jills are too large to enter the labyrinths that constitute the typical warrens of the brown rat. It has been argued that undersized hobs, hobs scarcely bigger than a tiny jill of the sort bred by Collingwood in the late 1950s (this was a popular strain of ratting ferret in the Midlands and Yorkshire at one time), would be equally as good at working rats as would a jill, but there is considerable evidence to suggest that this is not so. Large powerful hobs will often kill rats with great enthusiasm if rats can be found in places large enough for these hobs to work. However, if the sexual dimorphism that exists in wild polecats (and indeed in domesticated ferrets) is to allow both sexes an opportunity to exploit all available prey in a given area; then it is likely that the temperament, as well as the size of the two sexes, is vastly different and that jills are more likely to be prepared to take the battle to a rat-sized prey than would a hob. Conversely, it can be argued that the brown rat, the only suitable rat for a ferret to work, arrived in this country in the early 1700s when sexual dimorphism was already well-established in polecats and ferrets alike. However, if I might assume the role of devil's advocate: if the ferret is simply a domesticated form of the steppe polecat rather than the European polecat it seems likely that the ferret or rather the ancestors of the ferret (the steppe polecat) may well have encountered the Asiatic brown rat long before either species had been brought or migrated to Europe and the presence of the brown rat (rattus norvigicus) may well have added the dimorphism between the sexes of the steppe polecat. Whatever, hobs are less likely to want to tackle tough persistent rats than are jills, and prior to the 1911 Protection of Animals Act which afforded a somewhat fragile protection to even the brown rat few hobs were used in the rat killing contests staged near the Ship Inn, Leicester for Manship who kept the pit near the public house prior to 1912 found hobs had 'little stomach for the fight'.

On the subject of ferrets suitable for hunting rats, it is, perhaps, expedient to mention the greyhound ferrets once popular with terrier enthusiasts and commonly advertised by ferret breeders and dealers until the early 1960s when either the type, or perhaps merely the name, fell into disuse. Greyhound ferrets were found in all three colour phases – white, polecat and sandy, and were characterised by their long, slender but densely-muscled bodies. Some of the hobs were so long as to appear almost reptilian when they moved and many progressed with the back arching movements of a cartoon type mustelid. Tom Evans, one time rat catcher and springer spaniel breeder from Blaengarw, once stated that the very best greyhound ferrets were invariably white in colour, but Leslie Dyer of Cambridge, possibly the last person to advertise genuine greyhound ferrets, kept long greyhoundy polecat-coloured (some with lustrous mink-like black fitch fur) and sandy ferrets as well as whites. In addition to being of a slightly different shape, greyhound ferrets were supposedly more courageous than were rabbiting ferrets and survived ferocious battles with rats and had greater resistance to pain and sepsis.

It is likely that these ferrets were kept exclusively for ratting, for some were supposedly a little too quick and a lot too 'sharp' to allow rabbits to bolt.

What caused the greyhound ferret to pass into extinction – the greyhound ferrets advertised today are simply small white ferrets quite distinct from the ratting ferrets of post-war years until 1960 – is open to debate. My own opinion is that the decline of the rabbit from 1954 onwards following the outbreak of myxomatosis also reduced the saleability of rabbiting ferrets, and thus ferrets suitable only as warrener's ferrets were advertised as greyhound ferrets to hunters who pursued rats, now that the rabbit had been reduced to five per cent of its pre-myxomatosis numbers. Once the name of a product is abused and other products 'passed off' in its place the name of the original product soon passes out of use, and such was the case of the greyhound-type ferret – which is now seldom seen, even at ferret shows. I saw several dozen of these long, thin ferrets during my visit to Leslie Dyer's emporium in the late 1950s but saw only three male ferrets of this type when I visited Abbott brother's premises (the world's largest ferret breeders) prior to writing my book *Modern Ferreting*. I now believe that not only the name, but also the type, has passed into extinction and when I published this theory in *Shooting News* in 1990 not a single reader wrote in to dispute my claim.

Three distinct colour phases are found in ferrets though variations seldom exist in wild European polecats and even feral ferrets seem to revert to their fitch pattern in a very few generations. White ferrets, albinistic forms with white to cream fur and characteristic pink or red eyes, are apparently the most popular colour form with pet keepers and rabbiters/ratters alike. It is said that ferreters, both rabbiters and ratters, tend to favour white ferrets as they are easily seen as dusk begins to fall, a time when darker polecat ferrets and the diluted polecat ferrets, known as sandies, can pass unnoticed as they emerge from warrens. The claim that white ferrets are tamer than their more naturally coloured brethren is totally unsubstantiated and I believe that strain and constant handling produces tame ferrets rather than colour. The worst bites I have ever experienced from ferrets were inflicted by a particularly vicious pair of white kittens I had purchased from a breeder in Tamworth – a pair that refused to be handled or gentled by any means. Likewise, the most furious single bite I have received was from a dark polecat jill, ill fed and hungry perhaps, that would not release her grip when subjected to conventional methods and only relaxed her jaws when she was held in a barrel of water and nearly drowned before she opened her mouth to release my finger. I have owned both good and bad ferrets of each and every colour and while the current batch of ferrets I keep are white I confess I have a sneaking preference for dark fitch ferrets.

Dark fitch-coloured ferrets, virtually identical to wild polecats are often extremely beautiful animals, but there is no proof they are a whit superior, or inferior, to ferrets of other colours. I find the play faces of polecat ferrets particularly appealing and because of the unique facial markings manifested by this colour phase it is possible to detect the mood or disposition of a strange polecat ferret more easily than it would be to detect the mood of a white or cream animal.

In Germany, polecat ferrets were bred for their fur – sold as fitch – and Eartha Kitt, the singer, once caused great interest (and great furore) when she wore a coat made from fitch or ferret pelts during a tour of Great Britain.

It is interesting to note that feral ferrets – and whites, sandies and polecat ferrets often escape and revert to the wild, invariably revert to the polecat or fitch colouring of their wild ancestors after only a few generations. Trappers asked to remove feral ferret populations from remote areas seldom report either white or sandy feral ferrets appearing in their traps.

Sandy ferrets are simply pale, or diluted, forms of polecat ferrets and may vary in colour from nearly white with darker coloured tails – such a type is held in high esteem in Doncaster and surrounding areas at the time of writing – to nearly fitch-coloured animals a few tones lighter than wild polecats. Certain sandy ferrets closely resemble 'tourmaline'-coloured mink while other colour phases replicate other shades of marten or 'pale' sable fur. At one time Victorian rat catchers fought shy of using sandy-coloured ferrets as the colour phase had a reputation for cowardice, or to use the parlance of these rodent operatives 'quitting early', or refusing to face a rat once the ferret had sustained a bad bite or so. Once again, I have not found colour plays any part in the way a ferret performs against rat or rabbit and I have seen good, and not so good, sandy-coloured ferrets. One advantage the ferret keeper might experience, if he intends to work a large batch of sandy ferrets, is that as no two sandy ferrets are of exactly the same shade or hue, kits are easily recognisable from others. This is quite an important aspect of ferret keeping, I must add, as I know to my own cost. I keep a family of white ferrets and as I start out on a ferreting trip long before first light I usually reach into my ferret pen and take the first few ferrets that come to hand. It is extremely difficult to differentiate between white ferrets anyway and a month or so ago I was approached by a young ferreter from Kendal, who required a pair of working ferrets. I reached into my ferret pen and gave the young man two jills; only to discover a week later I had parted with my best working jill ferret. Had I kept dark polecats or sandy ferrets the difference between individual ferrets would have been instantly apparent – as it is one white ferret is almost exactly like another.

Thus, having dealt with the subject of sex colour phases and size of ferrets it is expedient to discuss how ferrets must be housed.

4

Housing

Over a period of years I have kept ferrets in a variety of coops, hutches, courts and cages and found them to be among the least demanding of all livestock. Providing ferrets are kept dry, given sufficient bedding to keep them warm, and a cage large enough for them to move their food away from their dung corner, ferrets will live and thrive in the most Heath Robinson of coops. I have seen litters of healthy kits reared in deep straw at the bottom of barrels, in packing cases, tea chests and even in an upturned four foot eighteen inch concrete pipe and the ferrets kept in these devices have been healthy and mentally well adjusted. I have also seen ferrets kept in open-sided mink cages, without bedding or shelter of any kind, and while these ferrets have lived in almost antiseptic conditions, for the dung fell through the grid wire floors, they were far from happy. I have, in fact, seen healthy ferrets reared in the most disgustingly dirty cages and observed that these ferrets are fit, healthy and free from the ailments that would have laid low most other types of livestock forced to live in such conditions. Hence I believe that ferrets need only to be kept dry, given bedding enough to ensure they do not chill and cages where their food does not become tainted with the ferrets own faecal matter. The elaborate cages suggested by most pet-keeping books are fine; aesthetically pleasing to the human eye perhaps and not an eyesore to prying neighbours, most of whom regard ferret keepers as slightly deranged, but such cages are no more efficient, no more functional, than a home-made cage that can be put together in a matter of hours.

My present cage is eight feet long, four feet high and four feet wide with three sides and a floor constructed of marine ply (which resists the rotting action of caustic ferret dung) with a grid wire front and a solid lid that lifts up to facilitate feeding, watering, handling and, occasionally, cleaning – and I confess that since I have had such a cage I have been fearfully remiss about cleaning out the dung corner until it becomes painfully apparent that I must before some plague unknown to virologists starts to infect the household and nearby crofts. Yet my ferrets thrive in such a cage, that is some two feet deep in loose straw under which my ferrets burrow and nest. The jills and my solitary hob are in pristine condition, tame and easily handled and live happy active lives climbing the wires and playing amongst the branches I have thrown in to act as play apparatus.

One point should always be borne in mind when one sets out to construct a ferret coop. The pen, coop or cage should be well enough constructed to be escape proof – and reader, to construct an escape proof ferret pen is no mean feat, for not only do ferrets find their way out of many home made pens, but they also find their way into any form of poultry pen and create havoc. Ferrets are clever enough at escaping to put a Houdini to shame and gaps and crevices, fit only to allow a mouse to escape will allow a ferret to find its way out of an otherwise escape proof ferret coop.

In the 1960s several companies patented galvanised steel multi-purpose small animal coops; pens suitable for housing a variety of small animals from guinea pigs to ferrets and while these cages proved extremely resistant to the dung and urine of small rodents the ferret excretia somehow corroded the cages in a matter of months and while such cages are still used by rabbit and cavy breeders, ferret keepers fight shy of using metal cages. At the time of writing Curtis Price, a professional fibre glasser from Powys, is investigating the possibility of constructing fibre glass cages specifically for ferret keepers. Fibre glass is virtually indestructible when subjected to normal use, easily repaired and resistant to the corrosive effect of ferret excretia. Sadly, such cages, while they will certainly last a lifetime are quite expensive to produce – though they are easily kept clean, resistant to even strong bleach and tough, even though they are extremely light.

Yet another suitable and easily cleaned material for the construction of ferret cages is the product *Stokboard* an easily cleaned, chemically resistant material that is composed of reconstituted plastic – a variety of plastic which may melt but not take fire even when subjected to very high temperatures. *Stokboard* is hard, tough, resistant, and while it is difficult to saw will take nails or screws without splitting. The material is virtually indestructible and the wood frames on to which the board can be fixed will rot and crumble to dust long before this reconstituted plastic becomes pitted. Hutches made from this material can be cleaned with boiling water or hot bleach solution without becoming corroded or warped. *Stokboard's* one and only disadvantage seems to be that, in common with the Ford Model T, it can be obtained in any colour

Jon Rodwell's purpose-built ferret pens

providing it is black. It is slightly more expensive than top class marine ply and totally non-absorbant, and this makes it an ideal material for the construction of ferret cages.

Yet wood is still the most popular material used to construct ferret coops hutches or pens, but this medium too has its disadvantages. Ferrets are all too inclined to become infected with a variety of illnesses and the bacteria and viruses that give rise to the ailments reside in porous wooden structures and become active whenever opportunity, temperature or new occupants to the hutch cause them to reactivate. It is often expedient to burn wooden hutches after a year or so of use and rebuild these hutches from fresh wood, particularly if the occupant of the hutch has suffered from intestinal complaints.

However, wooden hutches can be rendered more easily cleaned, and relatively disease free, if the woodwork is painted with a good quality water resistant paint. Ferrets seldom gnaw woodwork in the manner of a rabbit or a rodent and painted boards are rarely damaged by the scoring action of the claws of the ferret. Ferret dung is, however, extremely corrosive and destructive to both paint or metal and dung corners need to be scraped, washed and repainted if the woodwork is not to be destroyed by the combined action of ferret dung, and the bacteria that live in such faceal matter. In passing, it is wise to persuade and encourage a ferret to defecate in a convenient corner – a corner that can be easily cleaned – and, perhaps, reinforced with extra paint or metal corners that can be renewed from time to time. If a ferret is kept in a small box before it is introduced to its permanent home, and a quantity of its faecal matter daubed in a suitable corner of its hutch, the ferret will ever after use that corner as a latrine.

Whatever the material used to construct the ferret coop, a ferret must have a warm, sheltered corner of a hutch in which to sleep, and like most predators ferrets spend much of their time in sleep. A small wooden box with a tiny hole to allow the ferret to enter and leave its artificial lair is usually enough to keep a ferret healthy and happy, providing, that is, the box-like sleeping quarters are dry snug and draught free. Ferrets enjoy deep beds of straw, hay or, if these are unavailable, strands of heather or ling; but the constant shuffling action of a ferret prior to it bedding down usually reduces such material to fine shreds and thus the nest box bedding needs to be renewed every few weeks – though ferrets seldom, if ever, foul in or near their nesting quarters.

On the subject of hutches with wire floors – floors constructed of pea mesh, chicken wire, grid weld or twill weld – such floors allow urine, and some faceal matter, to fall through the gaps in the wire, and hence the hutches are usually dry and can easily be kept clean. Such hutches are very often quite cold unless the floors are covered with some thickness of straw or hay, and this material rather negates the use of a wire floor. Ferrets soon learn to run along these wire floors and seldom damage their feet on the floors of wire cages.

As to the size of the cage, this too is the subject of much debate. It can be argued that a huge cage, or a ferret-proof room, tightly sealed enough to prevent ferrets escaping would seem the right sort of abode for a ferret, or several ferrets, for such animals then have ample space to be able to exercise. This is patently true, for a ferret needs to be both fit and strong in order to endure a hard days rabbiting, or harder yet, a day's ratting. However, it should also be realised that ferrets are seldom as active as their wild ancestors and spend at least three quarters of their lives asleep. Yet, ferrets are never happy when kept in tiny coops in which they have no space to exercise or play – and ferrets allowed liberty spend much of their waking hours in play. Somewhere between the tiny ferret coop and the huge, roomy ferret court lies a happy medium. My own ferret pen is eight feet long, four feet wide and four feet high and allows ample space for ferrets to exercise and to feed away from their dung corner: but a hutch a yard long some two feet wide and two feet high is easily large enough to house one or two ferrets, particularly if those ferrets are given ample opportunity to exercise or to stretch their muscles by hunting.

On the subject as to whether a ferret thrives better if afforded company or kept singly, there is considerable evidence to suggest that ferrets not only tolerate, but prefer, a solitary life style. Polecats, the wild ancestors of ferrets, are naturally solitary – the male and female coming together only to mate while the female assumes the responsibility of single handedly rearing the young. It can be argued that domestication may have altered the habits of these polecats-cum-ferrets, but likewise, it should be mentioned that when two or more ferrets escape from captivity they seldom stay together. In 1967 a strong wind turned over my ferretry – a rather grand name for the huge chicken pen in which I kept my ferrets – and some twenty-four hobs and jills escaped. The tale has a rather horrendous note about it for I lived in chicken rearing country at the time, and while I recovered all but four of the ferrets by dint of box traps etc. (and the story of how I recovered some of my escapees would fill a large, though scarcely humourous book) I caught no two ferrets in the same vicinity and since that time I have never condemned anyone who kept a single ferret deprived of the company of its fellow mustelids. Ferrets are certainly more easily gentled if kept singlely – though I now believe there is a lot more to the production of tame friendly ferrets than simply handling them – and on this subject I shall say more later in the book.

How much light a ferret cage should afford its occupant or occupants is a moot point. I like open-fronted cages (the sides, top and bottom of which are of a solid structure) simply because I am usually remiss about cleaning out my ferrets with consistant regularity, and small stuffy cages certainly start to stink in a very short period of time if not cleaned regularly. Yet I have seen strong, healthy ferrets kept in dark and dingy hutches. When I lived in Rotherham I worked rat regularly and needed a large number of jill ferrets – and once again I shall explain why a ratter needs a large number of jill ferrets at a later stage in the book.

My search for new jill ferrets took me to one of those allotments that are scattered around the most unlikely quarters of industrial Yorkshire towns: allotments that often sport a variety of livestock ranging from the commonplace to the exotic. At one allotment I encountered a curious sort of man who kept, in addition to a huge variety of rabbits, tumbler pigeons and rather down-at-heel game fowl, a large crop of ferrets. His ferrets were housed in a large wooden shed in which no sunlight ever permeated and we viewed the ferrets he kept in a huge steel water tank by dint of a flash light. It would seem doubtful if these kits had ever seen daylight, and at the sight of the bright light arched their backs, hissed loudly and left the cadaver of the dead pig they were eating to investigate the lamp carrying intruders. Over thirty ferrets were housed in the water tank, nesting on deep if somewhat sticky straw and feeding on the corpse of a pig that had expired from one of the numerous ailments to which pigs seem all too prone. Some of the kits were a trifle undersized but were in good health, despite the fact they had never seen the sunlight and while they were a shade prickly for a week after I purchased them, I had no complaints about their working qualities despite the fact they were worked only at rat – the most testing quarry for any ferret. I hate leaving a tangle at the end of any anecdote; loose ends that leave a reader confused concerning the fate of the animals involved in the tale. The kits, or at least one of the kits, came with me to Lichfield and it was only during the curious outbreak of distemper in 1979 that I lost the last of these polecat ferret kittens. The line came to an end at the demise of this jill and her descendants and, frankly, I have never found ferrets good enough to replace them.

The structure and siting of doors, more than the amount of sunlight that can enter a ferret pen, determines how efficient the enclosure or cage is for ferrets are the very devil to escape and utilise any crack, crevice or weakness in a pen to effect their departure. I learned just how important doors were, and how important their construction was, somewhat late in life: during my mid-twenties in fact. At that time I kept a mess of ferrets (the correct collective name for ferrets) in an allotment adjacent to Holmes, keeping only jills and using the very tame polecat hob of a foundry worker everyone knew as Old Bill – I never discovered his surname. I learned quite a lot from this soft-spoken recluse, not perhaps about ferrets but about the diplomacy one needs to deal with the curious sort of person who keeps hunting dogs and allied animals. Bill's menagerie was housed in makeshift cages the doors of which were hung on hinges made from the leather 'tongues' of long discarded foundry boots. His ferret cage alone sported new and functional metal hinges. He explained that at one time he housed his ferret too in a Heath Robinson-type hutch, but the hob had escaped when the leather hinges rotted into nothingness and the ferret had caused havoc with a hatch of Sicilian Buttercup fowl he kept (I had not heard of the breed before or seen them since) after which Bill had been meticulous about the type of door used to restrain escapist ferrets. Tale has it that Bill was found dead on his beloved allotment – perhaps it is the way someone of Bill's ilk was meant to expire. He was the most contented man I have ever met.

Cage doors should fit snugly on ferret pens and the inmate should never be able to shake the door free or create a gap through which a ferret can escape. Cages that are fitted with hinged roofs, rather than conventional hinged fronts, are a nuisance to clean but the presence of these doors can cause chaos when ferrets race up the wire-netting to escape when the roof is lifted. A bar or plank of wood fitted some three inches on top of the netting wire front that will allow a ferret to crawl up the wire, but to become prevented from climbing out of the pen is an excellent idea and frankly one I had never considered before Curtis Price of Powys built me my present ferret pen. I have found this 'trap' plank invaluable, particularly since I live at the northern-most point of Great Britain and begin my ferreting day long before daylight reaching into my ferret pen and fumbling for the first jill to race up the wire front and wedge against the 'trap' plank. It is such a simple device, and so easily fitted, that I am bewildered as to why no one else has devised this method of construction. I hasten to add several friends have copied the idea when they have examined my ferret pen. Not once has a ferret escaped from this pen despite the fact that many times high winds have lifted the hinged roof of the pen. Before its construction I was forever hunting down ferrets that had escaped when conventional pens toppled by the winter winds had 'sprung' front fitting doors.

The positioning of a ferret pen is important, particularly if one wishes to breed ferrets in the cage. A ferret pen set in bright sunlight or in a position where a spell of sunlight can cause the pen to heat up can be a death trap to young kittens, particularly kittens that are in the process of starting to suck on solid food. Meat putrifies all too quickly in summer time and kittens eating such flesh bloat and die in hours. Ferret pens should always be stationed in a shady spot. My own pen is situated at a spot where bright sunlight (seldom a problem in Caithness) does not heat the pen in mid-summer or high winds (always a problem) do not chill the pen in mid-winter. Such a spot, adjacent to my dog kennel, is an ideal place for any ferret pen.

I am always sceptical about siting a ferret pen in a spot where ferrets can see or scent other small livestock – and I do not believe the proximity of a ferret helps the mental health of the small livestock either. Poultry certainly tend to take liberties with ferrets and dice with death when they attempt to peck at the food in a ferret's dish. Seldom is ferret cage mesh large enough to allow the heads of poultry to enter the cage, but chickens that attempt to filch food from a ferret pen often drive ferrets to frenzy. One of the worst bites I have ever received from a ferret was inflicted by a sandy jill quartered in the centre of a poultry yard where Leghorn-type hens stood on top of the ferret pen peering into the coop while a ferret fed on milk slop tried desperately hard to supplement its diet with raw and bloody poultry meat. I reached in to handle the jill shortly after I had driven hens from the roof of the ferret pen and the ferret driven crazy by the attentions of the chickens latched on to the flesh between my thumb and forefinger and endeavoured to shake off a fragment of flesh. I tried most methods to get the jill to release her hold finally holding her under the water in a rain water tank where midges bred and pond skaters darted to and fro. I am always amazed as to why I did not die from some horrendous disease during my spell in industrial Yorkshire. I have been bitten quite a few times by strange ferrets and each time I have attributed the bites to some irregularity in rearing or housing and not to some innate peculiarity on the part of the ferret.

5

Feeding

Ferrets were often described as ill-tamed polecats by early Victorian writers who were, often as not, more concerned with shotguns and shooting than with the finer points of bushcraft at which the artisan hunter often excelled. Yet while this description certainly does not do justice to the useful and usually friendly ferret it tells the stock keeper much of the dietary needs of a ferret. Ferrets kept on the type of viands eaten by their wild ancestors usually thrive and live to a fairly great age. Yet, having said this, the elderly polecat hob kept by Old Bill was fed a slop of bread and milk and lived to a great age – he was a great age when he served my mess of jill ferrets and never 'missed' a litter during my five year spell in Rotherham. However, I always attributed the hob's great longevity to the fact that, while the staple diet of the hob was deficient in both vitamins and protein, Bill's amazing variety of livestock, and the high death rate amongst his often geriatric fowl and rabbits provided abundant carcasses to supplement the hobs monotonous diet. Further-more, Bill's cage traps and his deadly break-back Nipper traps provided the hob with an abundance of rats once Bill's elderly terrier became too infirm to work.

The fact is that ferrets need meat, or meat substitutes, to thrive and prosper and it is curious that American city dwellers have such an affection for ferrets and keep the creatures in such splendid condition; that an English cottager would grow green with envy at the sight of such ferrets. The Americans have however always been streets ahead of us regarding the nutritional requirements of both animals and man, and while a request for a ferret mixture at a British pet shop would cause more than just a raised eyebrow from the shop assistant, such feed is available in America where mink, ferrets and other mustelids are popu-lar house pets. Most of the proprietary feeds available for the American keeper of mustelids are simply mink food compounds, feed geared and devised for keepers of pelt mink and are carefully compounded mixtures of meat offal (particularly liver) fish, soya, cereal with mineral and vitamin supplements added to the feed. While such foods are not readily available in Britain similar, though not identical, products are marketed as cat feed, cat pellets or other names and ferrets will thrive quite well on diets of well-soaked cat feed supplemented with the odd portion of fresh meat or road casualty cadaver.

Liver is the most popular feed bought for ferrets: either condemned liver, stained to prevent sale for human consumption, or butcher's liver bought for a fraction of the price of beef. Ferrets enjoy liver and will thrive on this offal – at least for a while. Aylcott noted that ferrets developed hypervitaminosis when fed exclusively, or almost exclusively, on liver and young kittens raised exclusively on liver developed spinal problems and hip joint deformities. The seal footed ferrets hind legs splayed out in the manner of a beached seal, once commonly seen at livestock markets, were probably the result of feeding kittens on an exclusively liver diet. I have seen similar disorders amongst ferrets fed exclusively on butcher's mince that is high in unpalatable fats and very low in calcium salts. Ferrets fed on such diets often benefit from a feed of milk or cat pellets soaked in milk, for such a diet supplies calcium to the growing kitten and adult alike. In 1965 a young man brought a huge batch of ferrets to sell at Doncaster livestock market and most of the kits displayed deformed hind legs. Frankly, while it is claimed that anabolic steroids and a correct diet will correct such deformities in a relatively short period of time, I would advise the reader to fight shy of buying such animals for healthy normal ferrets are readily available. To date I have reared only two kittens that manifested these peculiarities and I attributed this deformity to the fact that I had severely inbred my ferrets for ten or so years. Other litters reared on an identical diet displayed no sign of these deformities.

J.H. Lewington of the Craigie Veterinary Hospital in Western Australia is sceptical about using mink feed or dry cat food for ferrets except that is as an emergency standby diet when other food is unavailable. Mink, and neutered tomcats, fed on dry pelleted diets are notoriously susceptible to urinary calculi, stones of the kidney or gall bladder – though Lewington does not mention as to whether ferrets are susceptible to these disorders.

Canned dog meat or tinned cat food is a suitable, but very expensive, susbstitute for fresh meat, rodent and lagomorph flesh though some of the tinned dog meats have such a low protein level that cats seldom rear well if fed exclusively on these products. Tinned cat meats are usually much higher in protein; albeit fish protein that is not always acceptable to ferrets, but most ferrets, if allowed to miss a meal, find cat food palatable.

I have deliberately gone to some pains to suggest alternative feeds for ferrets simply because while it is best to attempt to replicate the natural diet of the wild polecat to feed ferrets, and rabbit meat seems to be the ideal food for young and mature ferrets alike, the time of year when ferrets need the greatest quantities of food (the time when kits will eat the ferret keeper out of house and home) coincides with the closed season for rabbit hunting, a time of year when it is morally irresponsible to hunt rabbits either by lamping (when rabbit kits will starve to death when milky does are caught by dogs) or by ferreting (for ferrets will readily kill and eat nesting rabbit kittens). Thus at the time of year when ferret food is most desperately needed it is least available, so alternative foods should always be at hand for the ferret keeper – particularly if that ferret keeper is rearing a litter of ferret kittens.

These days I set to and freeze down rabbit offal, myxomatosised rabbits and particularly rabbit heads that have fallen prey to my dogs and ferrets during the icy winter months in the Highlands, but my first season in the Highlands was a constant worry to me for I had two litters of kittens to rear and scarcely any suitable food to feed them. I learned to find substitute types of feed the hard way I am afraid and I would pounce on any road casualty cadavers with an enthusiasm that must have disturbed anyone who watched me. Rabbits, rats, a dead badger (and with the Badger Protection Acts of today being enforced at every opportunity by Badger Welfare Societies I would advise any hunter to pass by a dead badger at the roadside) vied with the corpses of gulls, rooks, and curlew and even two tawny owls and the remains of a rare short-tailed owl which brushed against a passing sheep-carrying wagon were tipped into my ferret cage. When a swarm of peltac (tiny pollack) swam into the bay they too were hooked and fed to my kittens, and dog fish caught in my nets were, at least for a while, eaten by my ferrets. I was fortunate enough to secure a box of monk fish; ugly black lagoon-type fish a tiny portion of the tail of which yields scampi (a shameful waste of the sea's resources) for £5 only to discover that my kittens had sickened of a piscean diet and rejected the ugly fish even when they were famished. Fortune favoured me late in July when the kittens, growing as though fed a diet conceived by H.G. Wells, were eating most heartily when the cadaver of a roe deer appeared on the roadside near my croft. The roe deer weighed roughly forty pounds and was scarcely a day dead but, despite the fact I froze down the meat, lasted a rather smelly five days before the kittens were bleating for food once again. During my stint in the Midlands I reared kittens on rats killed by my terriers – but my first year in the Highlands was made a nightmare by the appetites of my ferret kittens.

At the end of the summer when my efforts had succeeded in rearing a batch of twenty-five kittens (a litter of twelve and another litter of thirteen) I sat back and viewed the fruits of my labours one morning, gazing at the mess of ferrets that had exhausted me to feed. As I stood at the cage the phone rang and disturbed my reverie. I was jolted back to reality, made aware of the futility of my labours, by the voice of a livestock dealer who offered me fifty pence a piece for my kittens. The call could not have occurred at a less opportune time and my kits were homed with friends, free of charge rather than sell them to the animal dealer. In recent months ferret kittens are selling for fifteen pounds a piece – a realistic price when one considers the amount of food a growing ferret kitten will eat before it is old enough to part company with its dam. Enough however of economics and laments about the cost of rearing a litter of ferret kittens. These days I freeze down rabbit offal to last me through the summer months; but the reader must be fully aware how much it costs to rear a litter of ferrets. It is a financially prohibitive venture unless one has a readily available supply of fresh offal, or access to freshly deceased cadavers of birds or small animals from poultry farms or piggeries. Hence the would-be ferret rearer must always be aware of alternative suppliers of food.

The traditional feed for ferrets, both adults and kittens alike, was a diet of stale bread soaked in milk and providing this diet is sup-plemented with raw and bloody meat ferrets will survive on such a diet, but kits will not grow satisfactorily if they are kept exclusively on a slop feed. Ferrets fed such a diet and not offered fresh meat from time to time are prone to lie up on kills they make, for their bodies must literally crave the vitamins that are found only in the flesh of rabbits or rats. Rats or rabbits are often eaten by slop-fed ferrets and such ferrets will often lie up on their kills often glutting themselves with the flesh they have gnawed and stripped from their kills. A properly fed ferret is seldom as keen to indulge in persistent lie ups as is a ferret that is living on a slop diet.

I have often considered greaves or dried meat as a suitable alternative to fresh meat – that is if fresh meat is unavailable I should add. At one time the quality of greaves was poor and variable and ranged from leather-like strips to chunks of dried flesh that were in a state of decom-position long before the meat was processed. These days the drying and grinding processes have improved beyond belief. The flesh is not only thoroughly sterilised and hence free from the deseases that at one time made greaves dangerous to handle, but is now sold with an accurate break-down of its fat, protein, carbohydrate and vitamin levels. Ferrets scour, and scour quite badly when first introduced to large quantities of greaves, so it is policy to gradually introduce greaves to a ferret long before a meat crisis occurs so that if the ferret is put on an exclusively dried meat diet its condition does not plummet. Greaves is not a particularly palatable diet for ferrets but ferrets that are hungry will eat dried meat particularly if the greaves is soaked in warm milk for twenty-four hours before being offered as feed.

Many ferreters have some trepidation about feeding road casualty animals, but as the roads become increasingly overcrowded with traffic more and more small animals and birds succomb to the automobile and I am reluctant to waste good wholesome meat or see palatable cadavers of animals torn to slivers by passing cars. Drivers in the Highlands are often baffled as to why a great number of gulls fall victim to motor cars, but such birds are victims of their own insatiable appetites. Shortly after day break herring and black-back gulls scour the road for rabbit carcasses or the bodies of any other nocturnal animal that has been laid low by passing cars and such are the appetites of these gulls that they are reluctant to fly when a vehicle approaches them and then endeavour to flap incongruously into flight in front of the oncoming vehicles. A great number of black-back gulls grace the tarmac along the most northerly roads of Britain, and these too attract other gulls to their deaths. Ferrets will eat gulls of all kinds and will even feed on the oily guillemots that are trapped in the static nets of cod netters, but such gulls are surprisingly light and fleshless and ferrets gain little nourishment from a single bird.

Polecats, true wild polecats, will eat carrion readily, and some curious forms of carrion at that. There are reports of wild polecats stripping the meat from the carcasses of long dead road casualty badgers – curiously most mustelids are usually shy of killing or feeding on the carcasses of allied species (ferrets will usually disdain the flesh of stoats and weasels even if those ferrets have been fed on a meat-free diet for several months). Yet ferrets too will thrive on meat that is slightly too ripe. Though kittens suffer badly if their food is not absolutely fresh and die all too easily from botulism – a big killer of ferret and mink kittens. It is in fact better to feed kittens on a bread and milk diet for a day or so than chance allowing them access to meat that is suspect.

Eggs cracked open and left in their shells provide a good substitute for meat on days when fresh feed cannot be obtained but eggs should not be fed too often, particularly to kittens. There is some evidence that ferrets fed a surfeit of eggs suffer from Biotin deficiency, an ailment the symptoms of which are similar to follicular mange or perhaps alopecia. Some years ago a friend of mind, David Hancock of Sutton Coldfield, bred battery fowl and regularly gave me trays of cracked eggs to feed to both my ferrets and dogs. I saw not the slightest sign of alopecia or any other Biotin deficiency in either my ferrets or my dogs, but I feel I may have been lucky, or perhaps had the good sense to feed whole rats to the ferrets and only on the odd occasion did I feed them exclusively on raw eggs. However in 1981 I regularly hunted near Melton Mowbray and spent many days browsing around the small livestock market for which Melton is justly famous. Melton market has always been the place to visit to buy weaned ferret kittens in late July when the cost of rearing a litter is so high that breeders will dispose of surplus kittens for a song. That year I saw several scurfy kittens, and many with bare patches of reddened skin visible on their necks and back. These had been reared by a hunter who worked at an egg hatchery and I surmised he had fed his ferret kittens on a surfeit of infertile eggs – eggs candled at a week old and found not to be carrying an embryo chick. This, is I confess, the only time I have seem what could possibly have been a Biotin deficiency in ferrets.

On the subject of vitamin deficiency an abundance of uncooked oily fish in the diets of dogs, mink and silver foxes will often produce a peculiarity known as Chasteks paralysis. Fish contains an enzyme called Thiaminase which destroys the vitamin Thiamin and hence produces a peculiarity known as Chastek's paralysis. Animals afflicted with this peculiarity lose weight rapidly, develop a jerky gait and finally become paralysed and die. Mink and silver foxes are particularly susceptible to this disorder but I have observed symptoms of the sort described in a kennel of pointers and setters, the owner of which had access to an abundance of salmon waste. Ferrets, contrary to popular opinion, will eat fish readily at first but after a while pall of the diet and refuse to so much as carry pieces of fish to their nest boxes. I have always considered that this was an indication that I was feeding too much fish and once I have observed this behaviour I have changed the diet of the ferrets immediately. I have never observed an illness similar to Chasteks paralysis in my ferrets despite the fact that my ferrets have been fed on the most varied diet imaginable. At one time I had access to corpses, animal corpses I must add, from a livestock importer (I am fairly sure she should have burned the cadavers and not given them to my ferrets to eat) and my ferrets have dined on a variety of exotica ranging from penguins to puma cubs and perhaps because of the variety of strange meats my ferrets ate I reared some of the best kittens I have ever seen. Anyone who has had the problem of rearing many litters of ferret kittens becomes a veritable 'snapper-up of unconsidered trifles'.

As to the quantity and quality of food a ferret needs; it has been suggested by Lewington that ferrets need a diet that is richer in protein than the diet prescribed for feeding mink. Mink will exist and grow fairly well on a diet of twenty-five per cent protein (mammalian, avian and piscean protein). Indeed in the post-war years mink were kept on a diet of twenty per cent protein but the optimum protein level for mink seems to be between twenty-five and thirty-four per cent. Fitch farmers who breed polecat and sometimes sandy ferrets for their pelts tend to feed a diet that is roughly forty per cent protein (four to six ounces of good quality animal protein per ferret per day) which lends a lie to the notion that ferrets will function on a diet of bread and milk (a protein level of perhaps less than twelve per cent). It is thus all the more baffling that for centuries ferrets have been maintained on bread slop rations and have reared kittens on such appalling diets.

6

Breeding

The curious breeding habits of all mustelids have amazed and confounded naturalists since the days of Aristotle. Weasels, or the presence of weasels, around the houses of Magyar farmers were believed to indicate the sexual potency of the master of the house while the steppe polecat, the ancestor of the domesticated ferret perhaps, was regarded as a symbol of sexual infidelity by some of the nomadic tribes people of Southern Russia. Truth is invariably stranger than fiction or legend as the scandalous socio- sexual life of the male stoat attests.

Both polecats and ferrets are extremely vociferous during coition and both male and female (particularly the female) chatter loudly during mating. Copulation lasts for an hour, or slightly less, but Sleeman records that domesticated ferrets will couple noisily for up to two-and-a-half hours. This lengthy period of mating (as opposed to the relatively brief courtship of the wild ancester of the ferret) is said to be due to the fact that, once a wild polecat has been served, she seeks to escape the attentions of the male though this explanation does not explain the lengthy mating ritual of ferrets. Captive ferret jills are afforded no such opportunity to escape confined as they are by hutches, and are often served time and time again by vigorous males. Yearling male ferrets are particularly virile and if restricted to serving merely one jill may spend most of the day serving her repeatedly and quite often damaging the jill unless she is allowed to retreat to a spot where a hob cannot follow. Hobs allowed or encouraged to serve many jills often start to decline physically as many might neglect to feed while there are female ferrets to mate. Virile hobs kept in colony conditions will often fight and subdue inferior hobs and attempt to serve them, and sometimes inferior hobs will die when they are repeatedly badly mauled by a sexually vigorous male ferret.

The study of the breeding habits of wild polecats will tell the ferret keeper much of the needs of his domesticated wards. Wild polecat females establish hunting territories that are smaller than the territories of the males and in the mating season seek out and allow male polecats to serve them, but then after mating escape the attentions of the male and retreat to the security of their own territory. Male polecats defend their territory vigorously against invading males (and also against females during the winter months when the females are sexually unresponsive) and noisily attack intruders of the same species and gender.

The behaviour pattern of wild polecats during the mating season should ilustrate numerous points regarding the type of stock husbandry required of those who endeavour to breed ferrets. Firstly the process of putting a jill in a cage with a vigorous and amorous hob is obviously not an advantageous one – particularly for the jill who cannot escape the attentions of a very vigorous yearling hob. Thus once the hob has mated the jill, and the lengthy noisy mating session may last for over an hour, the jill is best taken from the hob to allow her at least some respite from the constant mauling she receives from her mate. Every alternate day the jill should be put back into the hob's cage to be served yet again until she is coming off season after which no further marital visits will be either efficacious or necessary. Jills should be taken to the hob and allowed to mate in the hob's cage, or in a place that is well known to the hob, for apparently wild polecat females will leave their well-established territory to seek out mates. Hobs should be allowed to mate only a few females each season and the use of vasectomised hobs (hobs deliberately sterilised but still with their sexual desires undiminished) should be carefully regulated lest the hob exhaust himself by repeatedly serving a large number of females in order to render them 'off season' but not pregnant – and this subject will be dealt with presently. Polecats are solitary creatures, the sexes coming together only during the brief mating period: hence if Renz Waller the falconer was correct in his assumption, to breed domesticated animals and birds the stock keeper should do his best to allow his wards to live the life style of their wild ancestors. While some hobs take to living with females before, during and after the pubation of the female the process is unnatural and may well create tension, trauma and psychological disturbance for both hob and jill and possibly the kittens – and I shall deal with the subject presently. Thus Waller's notions concerning the breeding of animals and birds that have only recently been subjects of domestication – and it seems likely that the ferret has evolved from its wild polecat ancestor only in the last three thousand years – and reverts to its wild ways easily and predictably if allowed to lead a feral existence.

Jill ferrets are photo-periodic breeders – they come into season as the days begin to lengthen during spring or early summer. In fact it seems likely that increasing periods of light, rather than a rise in temperature, may induce a jill ferret to start her oestral cycle. An article or letter appeared in *Shooting News* in the 1980s and suggested that ferrets might be brought into season at any time of the year if kept in a shed and subjected to artificial light. I have yet to see any factual evidence to substantiate this premise but if extra light is given to a ferretry for several weeks from mid-winter onwards for a few minutes per day on 21 December and is increased by perhaps five extra minutes per day, ferrets may well come into season earlier than they would if kept outside and given no extra light. However one must question as to whether it is advantageous to breed early ferret kittens anyway and frankly there seems to be very little advantage to be gained by the production of very early kittens, for kittens produced in the early days of summer (without the use of artificial light) are usually big enough, strong enough and mature enough to work rabbits as soon as the first frosts make it practicable to ferret. As a jill ferret comes into season her vagina swells and becomes turgid and may swell to become the size of a woman's thumb nail and, if not mated, jills may stay in this condition for the entire summer. It was often believed that if jills were not mated they were prone to die, but while this is not always the case some jills will lose weight become emaciated, lose fur and body condition (and look positively wretched by the end of the season). Indeed some jills, if not mated become so debilitated that they may not recover. Other jills come into season, remain in season for what must seem an inordinate length of time, but suffer no effects from this lengthy oestrus.

Why jills die if not mated, or what is the reason why jills will become ill and emaciated has long been the subject of debate by veterinary surgeons. At one time I had every jill that had died after a lengthy period of staying in season autopsied and in each case the wall of the uterus of the affected jill was found to be inflamed and infected with some form of staphylococcus or streptococcus infection. Lewington suggests another reason why such jills fall ill, become emaciated and die however, for he believes that once the endocrine system of an in-season ferret goes awry post oestral anaemia may contribute to the ultimate decline of the jill.

At the same time as the vulva of the female starts to enlarge, the testicles of the mature hob become noticably apparent and the males become slightly more aromatic than usual. It is believed that, in the wild, a female polecat or feral ferret will actively seek out a wild male and detect his presence by the hob's strong scent. For this reason it is wise to take a female to the male ferret rather than vice versa. These peculiar scent glands are present in both sexes, but are more acutely developed in the male and the presence of these pungent scent glands have given the ferret its specific and generic names: Mustela Putorious – the evil smelling musk carrier.

The hob serves the jill with great vigour grasping the female by the nape of the neck and penetrating her with furious thrusts. The female may chatter and scream frantically, and hence tyro ferret keepers may be concerned for the welfare of the jill. This ritual however is essential for the furtherance of the species and unless the hob and jill complete the rituals of this ceremony to the letter, the jill may not ovulate and conceive. Ovulation occurs between thirty and thirty-six hours after mating and once conception has occured the female's vulva becomes flaccid and decreases in size resuming its normal shape and dimensions some ten days later. A female that is not served remains in season and the tissue of the females genitalia can become damaged and infected. Hence it is vital to ensure that even if the jill does not conceive she must be mated so that the vaginal swelling will subside. Ferret keepers who wish to keep jill ferrets, but not be burdened with the rearing of a litter of kittens therefore resort to the use of a vasectomised hob – an ingenious deception that allows the jill to be mated but not to conceive.

It is only in recent years that the use of a vasectomised hob has been practised, but the use of such a male has much to commend it. Vasectomy is a simple operation, but one that must be conducted by a qualified veterinary surgeon (and should never be undertaken by a lay practitioner). The operation, which incidentally is irreversible, involves the severing of the vas deferens, the duct that connects the testes to the penis, and thus the hob, while it retains its libido, is unable to impregnate the jill. It should be pointed out that there is a marked difference between the processes of vasectomy and castration. Castration involves the removal of the testicles and thus a castrated hob is not only infertile, it also displays little or no inclination to serve a female. Many ferret clubs employ the use of a vasectomised hob which is passed amongst the members to ensure jills are mated but no unwanted surplus kittens are produced. Vasectomised hobs should be treated with respect though they are frequently overused. The hob is not a machine capable of copulating without respite. Hobs that are over used, mated far too often to far too many jills often lose weight and can die from excessive exertion. A wild polecat seldom mates a great number of females though it may cover and mate half a dozen females if the females are available, and the wild polecat is living in country that will provide a suitable diet for several polecats. Vasectomised hobs should never be left for several days with an in-season female, but rather should be put in with the female perhaps every other day until the female's vulva becomes flaccid which indicates she is no longer in season. A hob used in this manner will copulate with perhaps ten or twelve jills, but a hob used to this extent should be well-fed and well-housed.

However if kittens are required, a vasectomised hob should not be used for while the animal may mate with a jill the female will not produce kittens after such a union. Thus only an entire and healthy unvasectomised hob should be used for the production of kittens. Very large powerful aggressive hobs must be used with care lest they damage the female but dangerously sexually active hobs are rare. Only once have I encountered a hob that was really dangerous with jills. Some years ago I owned a polecat hob that I used as a line ferret. He was a delight to own and gentle as a lamb when handled. However with other ferrets, both male and female, he was vicious and would attempt to mate with either sex, even during winter months when male ferrets are seldom sexually active. No ferret would continue to lie up if this hob was put to ground behind them, and both jills and hobs emerged tails in gales when this hob found them lying up on a kill. I have never since owned a hob that was his equal as a line ferret, but he mauled jills so badly that I never managed to produce kittens by him. He attacked in-season jills furiously endeavouring to kill rather than serve them. I left him unattended but once with a jill and her screaming, quite distinct from the mating sounds and chattering emitted by a normal copulating female, alerted me to the deed the hob was perpetrating. I raced to the hutch to find him biting the head of the female and the hutch wreaking of the stench of a very frightened ferret (normally jills do not emit this scent while mating). I managed to separate the pair (it is usually possible to lift mating ferrets without them separating) but the jill was so terrified she struck at my hands. I tried to mate the hob with a dozen or so jills but he attacked and mangled each and every potential mate so fiercely that I decided not to use him to breed. It was a pity for had he replicated his qualities in his kittens I would have bred excellent line ferrets – and this term will be explained presently. Sadly, he met his end when his hutch blew over in a gale and a motor vehicle struck him when he attempted to cross the road near my cottage. I never saw his like again and I now consider his behaviour to be aberrant and certainly not typical of the behaviour of most hob ferrets.

Once the jill has ceased to be in season, and may or may not be in kindle, it is wise to separate the jill from the hob. Some hobs will actively help rear a litter, cleaning the bellys of the kits and dragging the young back to the sanctuary of the nest when the young stray out of the nest or are carried out adhering to the jill's nipple. Such behaviour is certainly not typical of male ferrets in general for many hobs are fiercely cannibalistic and devour kits (particularly newly born blood-stained kits) and it is wise not to allow a hob near young baby ferrets. Female polecats not only nest as far from the hob's territory as possible but often chose lairs the entrances to which are too narrow to allow a hob access to the nesting chambers.

Perhaps at this juncture it is necessary to mention once again why hobs are so much larger than typical jills. The subject of sexual dimorphism is one that is hotly debated by naturalists. Male stoats are scarcely bigger than bitch stoats: polecat males are considerably larger than females of the same species. However the difference between the sizes of male and female mustelids is never more pronounced than amongst fishers, medium sized mustelids, the females of which are a mere four pounds in weight, while the males are a massive twelve pounds – the size of a small vixen. It is often stated that female polecats will prey on somewhat different quarry from the quarry hunted by the larger more powerful male and the Erlinge Moors hypothesis has already been explained earlier in the book. Yet another suggestion to explain their sexual dimorphism might be that male polecats have a tendency to be cannibalistic, and that the smaller size of the female allows her to be able to nest in places where hobs find it difficult to invade. Female stoats however are smaller than males of the same species yet male stoats show no cannibalistic tendencies towards their young, despite their curious sexual habits. Whatever the reasons for the disparity in size between male and female ferrets and polecats there is considerable evidence to suggest that a hob ferret has no place in the nursery cage with the female and her young.

The gestation period of the ferret varies between forty-two to forty-nine days, and the variation in the gestation period can be explained by the fact that ovulation occurs up to thirty-six hours after mating. Some jills will kindle some forty-two days after mating while others produce young up to fifty days after they are introduced to the hob. Jills will often breed two litters of kittens per year, particularly if an early litter suffers some mishap and dies before weaning. It is seldom wise to attempt to breed two litters a year from a jill ferret however. Kits are seldom easy to sell and late bred kittens are rarely old enough to work until half way through a rabbiting season. Furthermore, jills that still have a suckling litter at home will rarely give of their best when rabbiting, and certainly not while ratting when an injury is more than likely to incapacitate a suckling jill. One litter of kittens per season is usually more than enough for a jill to rear.

Jills with tiny, newly-born kittens should be left in peace, and dogs, children and other possible annoyances kept well clear of the breeding cages. Some jills, even otherwise tame, easily handled jills, will bite furiously when their young are handled or when the ferreter even touches the nesting area. Many ferreting books state that jills will allow the ferreter to handle the young kits soon after the jill has kindled, but to attempt to handle the kits at this stage is an unwise action. Even the tamest jill may react savagely if she feels her young are threatened or her privacy is being violated. Some years ago I owned an extremely good ratting ferret I called Fudge. She would face the most ferocious doe rat, but allow me to handle her as soon as she came away from the affray. She came to hand when called, retrieved a paper ball when I played with her in my tiny kitchen, and deliberately sought me out if she lost me during a day's ferreting. Yet when Fudge kindled she would menace me if I attempted to put food in her pen and attack me if she considered I kept my hand in her cage for an unnecessarily lengthy period of time.

Both ferret and wild polecat kittens are born naked, blind and help-less and remain blind for as long as thirty-five days after birth. Puppies and kittens open their eyes when they are ten days old. Ferret kittens remain totally blind until thirty to thirty-five days of age and are able to focus on objects a few days later. This peculiarity, common to all mustelids from fishers to weasels, has attracted the interest of zoologists since the time of Gilbert White *Natural History of Selbourne*. It is be-lieved that this lengthy period of blindness restricts a precocious species of animals to the nest, preventing the very young animals from wander-ing abroad until they are old enough to deter and threaten a potential attacker. Very young polecats, and feral ferrets some thirty or so days old, will hiss and threaten anyone attempting to handle them and endeavour to bite with their tiny needle-like teeth even though their jaws are not strong enough to inflict hurt. It is also of interest to note how upset and agitated jills become when young kittens with their eyes not yet open stray from the nest. Jills allowed to nest communally, a cheap but not a beneficial system of breeding ferrets one should add, will often become disturbed when they find adult jills leaving the nest to feed, urinate or defecate and will rush out, seize the jill and endeavour to haul her back to the sanctuary of the nest. Whether or not this is a compulsive reaction to retrieve creatures leaving the nest, is instinctive or whether the reaction is accentuated by compelling ferrets to nest in unnatural conditions – colony breeding certainly does not simulate the conditions under which polecats would nest – has yet to be ascertained.

It is almost inevitable that if a jill ferret, a descendant of the polecat, an animal with a solitary disposition, is forced to live and nest in the very unnatural conditions experienced in colony breeding projects, the jills will react strangely. Jills may choose to nest some distance from each other: when a nesting jill hears the squeaking of the kittens of another litter she often becomes distressed and deliberately seeks out the kits and carries them to her nest. The other jill, equally distressed, follows the thief to the nest and either attempts to retrieve her stolen kittens or remains with both litters in the communal nest. Mortality amongst kittens reared in such a manner is unacceptably high, particularly if one litter is a week or so older than the second litter and can push aside the smaller kits when they attempt to suckle. It is in fact highly unlikely that many of the younger litter will survive the 'adoption'.

The need for jills to carry any squeaking, squealing kittens to the nest has been utilised by several naturalists who have attempted to rear young orphaned weasels, stoats, mink, polecats and even martens alongside ferret kittens. The orphaned kittens are usually placed on the far side of the pen that houses a nursing jill ferret and the alien mustelids allowed to become chilled just long enough to cause them to squeak. The sound distresses the jill who comes to investigate the bleating cry of the kittens and she will usually carry them to her nest – though it is not unknown for the jill to eat the kittens of other mustelids. This tendency to carry back young animals that are bleating piteously was exploited by keepers of travelling menageries prior to the 1900s when regulations evolving from ramifications of the 1911 Cruelty to Animals Act and the formation of the Jack London Clubs after 1917 brought an end to many of the techniques used by travelling circuses and peep shows. Ferrets with nursing kittens were deliberately fed nests of young live rat kittens, naked kittens for preference, but sometimes fully furred ratlings. In all probability the jill would kill and eat the majority of the kittens, but some she would probably carry to her nest where, mingling with the scent of the ferret kittens, the ratling would be overlooked and adopted by the normally hostile ferret. It was not uncommon for menageries to sport messes of young ferrets in the midst of which a young rat cavorted and was accepted by its ferocious foster brothers and sisters. Early writers of books concerned with ferrets often remarked on this phenomenom but the exhibit was commonly seen at Black Country fairs prior to 1911. Further interest would be generated by the show man by tipping live rats into the cage where upon both ferrets and foster Judas ratling would attack and dismember the new rat. These macabre acts were very popular in the Black Country where the twin lure of ratling and ferrets attracted huge crowds. After the prosecution of Manship at Leicester in 1912 (a prosecution erroneously referred to as the Ship Inn Prosecution) rat killing acts of any sort fell out of favour in Britain.

However, to return to the subject of ferret breeding. Kits leave the nest even before their eyes are open to suck meat or milk sop, particularly if the jill is short of milk or if the litter is excessively large. It is at this time that mortality amongst kits is likely to be at its highest and there are few ferret keepers who cannot tell stories of litters of ferrets which have mysteriously become bloated and died during this weaning period. Many reasons are proffered to explain these deaths – and the problem also troubles breeders of ranch mink. Autopsies of kittens usually reveal enlarged spleens and damage to the kidney tissues. Lewington attributes these deaths to excessive summer heat, a cold snap at night, flea infestation and possibly an infection with a virus. He also reports streptococcus traces in the blood taken from the hearts of some of these kittens. However most of the kittens that died in my ferretry, when I lost a large number of kittens in 1982, were autopsied and my veterinary surgeon suggested that some form of botulism was responsible for their deaths. Many old time ferreters were loathe to feed anything but still warm rabbits or rats to kits and promptly removed the chewed carcasses once both jills and kits had fed well lest the meat began to get 'high' and toxic to the youngsters. Meat which is perfectly acceptable to adult ferrets (stale and often putrifying flesh) will be lethal to kittens that are in the process of being weaned.

The amount of food consumed by a litter of growing ferrets is collosal and a first time ferret breeder will often be astonished to find that what he considers to be a quantity of food suitable for a growing litter is consumed in seconds and the kittens still appear famished. It is estimated that an average-sized jill ferret needs a maintenance ration of roughly six ounces of minced meat to which has been added a pinch of fine bone meal or dicalcium phosphate. A young ferret kitten just leaving the nest and beginning to take solid food may consume an ounce of flesh, but once the kitten is fully weaned and ceased to suckle the dam, the youngster will need nine or ten ounces of food in order to grow to its optimum size. Thus a jill with a litter of ten kittens, and many jills will breed and rear twelve or more kittens, will need six ounces of meat to maintain the jill and ten ounces of meat for each of the ten young kittens – a total of one hundred and six ounces of meat, six-and-a-half pounds of mince meat – a considerable quantity of meat by any standards particularly if the ferret breeder has to buy, even cheap, pet mince at ten pence a pound – perhaps fifty pence per day or £3.50 per week. Hence it is not really profitable to rear litters of ferrets on a diet of pet mince and sell the kittens for perhaps £1.00 apiece. If one wishes to feed such a diet, and sell the kittens at a price that will allow the ferret keeper to break even or make a slight profit, then the costing of the project is rather frightening.

Maintenance ration for a jill for 52 weeks at 42 ounces of meat per week at 10p per pound equals 52 x 10 x 2⅝ lb of meat or £13.60 per annum. Ten kits fed for 4 weeks at 10 ounces per day each, on the same diet, would work out at roughly £10.00 to cover the cost of food. Thus, to rear a litter could cost out at as much as £23.60 or perhaps £25.00 would be a more realistic price for rearing a litter of ferrets and the maintenance of the jill for a year. Thus to merely clear the ferreters expenses, kits would need to be sold at £2.50 each. This costing, rough and inaccurate as it is, should give the ferret keeper some idea of how to price the cost of his kittens. It can however be argued that if the jill is worked to rabbit or rat throughout the season (and ratting ferrets are worked summer and winter alike) the jill can be maintained virtually free of charge – simply by feeding the jill on the rabbit waste and, if the ferret keeper has tolerant neighbours, on the cadavers of healthy rats. So let us estimate that if the jill is maintained free of charge the litter would still perhaps cost only £10.00 to rear but this assumes bedding and occasional drinks of milk can be obtained free of charge. In 1991 ferret kittens well reared on a meat and milk diet, were advertised at £15.00 each and frankly this would be a fairly realistic price for a well-reared kitten. However here the supply and demand factor now enters the costings. A ferret kit may well be worth the £15.00 asked for it (and perhaps the lot of the ferret would be better than it is if it was sold for a higher price) but a visit to a livestock market will usually find dozens of disenchanted ferret keepers (some of whom probably believed they would get rich breeding ferrets) who, having been reduced to penury by the cost of rearing a litter, are attempting to sell their kits in a market that is choc-a-bloc with surplus ferret kittens. When such a surplus is offered for sale there is a distinct likelihood that the kits will be sold off for pence rather than pounds. At Melton in 1986, shortly before I left for Scotland, I saw a mess of ferret kits sold as a job lot for 25p each. They were in excellent condition and if I had needed ferrets at that time I would certainly have bought them. They handled well, were healthy, clean and inquisitive and a great deal of love and labour went into the rearing of these kittens, yet they were sold for a fraction of the price they cost to rear.

Field sportsmen are often damnably short sighted about the stock they keep and, if I reared such a litter, I would have suffered a few weeks more penury and offered them for sale at the start of the rabbiting season when for some reason ferrets are usually in short supply and command high prices – and while it must seem absurd to the more sophisticated town dweller that there are bulls and bears in even the ferret market it is often the case. At one time it was common to find livestock dealers who kept a variety of livestock and sometimes had a high mortality rate amongst their stock – buy up hundreds of surplus ferret kittens, feed them on the cadavers of fallen stock and then sell the ferrets in mid-September for a handsome profit. The ferrets fulfilled two purposes. Firstly they gained value at an incredible rate in a matter of weeks and secondly they ate up dead fowl, piglets and calves which would otherwise have to be buried or burned. If the kits were 'bought gentle' and maintained on a good diet they stayed gentle and could be sold as trained ferrets – for a single trip out in September renders a healthy kit trained after a fashion – and I must stress 'after a fashion'. At one time a brief eight week period in a large ferret court could push the value of a ferret from 50p to £6.00 or £7.00 and should the town dweller scoff at this profit margin it represents a gain that would make a Wall Street speculator green with envy – 8400% per annum. Tony Richards, a horse dealer from East Anglia in the 1970s, often reared a huge crop of ferrets during the summer months touting them around the livestock markets when the task of rearing ferrets became a shade odious, not to say expensive. Richards, astute and as gifted with epigrams as most horse dealers seem to be, stated that had he suitable premises and an abundant supply of casualty livestock it would have been more lucrative to deal in ferrets than in horses. Feeding ferrets on fallen livestock probably represents one of those shadowy areas touched on by the 1936 Public Health acts, but ferrets reared on such diets seldom seem to suffer from the diseases one would expect from animals kept on such a diet.

Ferret dealers who buy cheap and sell dear – and that is the nature of all trade – usually keep their kittens in purpose-built courts; brick-built cubicles under cover of Dutch barn roofs and bedded on deep straw. If the straw becomes fouled, fresh straw is tipped on top of the old bedding until the level of the straw reaches the point where ferrets can escape from the courts. Yet despite this seemingly insanitary method of keeping livestock, ferrets seldom suffer from any ill effects of such deep litter systems and some of the finest ferrets I have ever seen were reared in these courts.

If I might return to the subject of unmated jills a moment. If jills are kept adjacent to vigorous and pungent hobs they will often stay in season only a short time despite the fact that they are unmated. Ferret breeders often report this phenomenon and note that the jills often appear to be pregnant in spite of the fact that they have had no opportunity to be served. Pseudo- pregnancies of this kind are far from uncommon in the animal kingdom and most mustelids, frustrated by the proximity of a pungent male, will display symptoms of this peculiarity.

Kittens should be handled literally from the nest or as soon as they leave the nest, though jills are often so protective with young kittens

White hob ferret

that the ferreter will often need to employ a subterfuge in order to be able to lift a kitten from the nest. Frequent handling usually ensures that ferret kittens are gentle – and spiteful ferrets can be nightmares to own. I have related the tale of a pair of bought-in ferret kittens that refused to be gentled in *In Pursuit of Coney* so I will not repeat the story, but I believe most of the faults displayed by adult ferrets offered for sale in mid-winter (and the reader should always treat the sale of adult ferrets with some suspicion) are due to lack of handling or bad handling in the nest.

The worst of the handling techniques is rather jokingly referred to as 'strangling' or gripping the ferret kitten by the throat allowing the body to hang earthwards. Ferrets dislike being handled so and consequently struggle to be free of such a grip. Now the strangler, who is secretly afraid of ferrets (hence the grip which keeps the ferret's mouth well away from his hand), interprets this struggling as an indication the ferret is about to attack and grips tighter thereby creating a vicious circle effect which finishes up with the hitherto very tame kitten biting like a fury to be free of the maniac who is attempting to throttle it. What is worse is that a strangler, who has provoked a kitten to bite him (the strangling malaise is seldom encountered amongst women), becomes even more afraid of handling ferrets and if made to pick up a ferret will ever after adopt the strangle-hold technique despite the fact that he has observed the same kittens handled with impunity by ferreters who lift a kitten by dint of a gentle hold behind the fore legs of the creature. A strangler not only sets a seasoned ferreter's teeth on edge but can sour an entire litter of kittens that, before being badly handled, were vice free. A seasoned strangler, and a strangler will invariably claim to have been taught his skills by an old poacher (Victorians often hanged poachers and if these poachers taught their acolytes ferret strangling there is much to say for Victorian justice) can cause the tamest ferret kitten to hiss in anger when lifted by a ferreter and stranglers, or those who adopt the strangling technique, should never be allowed to touch ferrets. Few will object to the ban, for the strangler has a secret fear of ferrets and is only too willing to allow others to handle them.

The very worst strangler I have ever encountered was a young man from near Glasgow who had cultivated the technique of strangling to such a level that he could take the most gentle of ferrets and produce a furious hissing vicious brute in minutes. Ray, for so the gentleman was called, was quite a pleasant person who had an unfortunate way with ferrets. At the time I knew him I had a very tame white hob ferret which allowed the daughters of a friend of mine to dress him in doll's clothes and the hob seemingly enjoyed the indignity. I never saw the hob threaten, let alone bite, but in a single hour with the creature Ray succeeded in provoking the hob to draw blood on Ray's best throttling hand.

Alas Ray manifested other handling peculiarities. Yet another even more upsetting habit than throttling is the malaise often referred to as juggling – and kittens subjected to even a brief stint of juggling are difficult to handle for weeks after the experience. A juggler, one who perpetrates the act of juggling, is also secretly terrified of ferrets and as kittens often attempt to play bite, displaying the play face expression that tells the experienced ferreter that he is not in any sort of danger – the juggler usually performs at his best, or worst, depending on how one regards the spectacle with impressionable kittens and the expression 'spectacle' is more than justified. If the ferreter is able to stop the juggler in mid-term so to speak, a juggler is fascinating to watch though very destructive to the manners of the kittens. A competent ferret handler will reach in and gently lift a ferret kitten despite the playful antics of the kittens that may be dancing, jaws open, but offering no threat to the handler. A juggler behaves somewhat differently when faced with the same situation. He will usually reach into the cage gingerly, only to withdraw his hand should a kitten attempt to engage him in play. After a moments respite the juggler will usually attempt another assault on the kitten who, believing the juggler wishes to play, treats the approaching hand with a curious dance and a play-face expression. The juggler who has neither a liking for, nor a knowledge of, ferrets is alarmed by the play response of the kitten and once more withdraws his hand, a shade more quickly than hitherto one must add. The kitten, now mystified and perhaps slightly alarmed by the behaviour of the juggler, ceases to play and becomes suspicious of the hand that now starts to approach the kitten from yet another angle. In minutes the kitten will become disturbed, puzzled and hostile to the hand that approaches, then retreats only to come at the ferret from yet another angle. I always suspect that neurotic ferrets are the result of mishandling more than bad breeding.

A kitten should enjoy being handled and should never strike at the hand that is reaching towards it. It should experience pleasure at being touched and should greet the appearance of the ferreter with delight rather than by skulking back into its sleeping quarters when the ferreter approaches its cage. I should be decidedly wary of attempting to handle a ferret that withdrew into the sanctuary of the darkness of its cage when I attempted to touch it. I am a shade casual about the way I handle my own ferrets possibly because of my peculiar lifestyle. I begin my day's hunting before first light and after touching the side of the cage to wake my ferrets I reach into the cage and fetch out the first ferrets to race up

A well-behaved ferret is a delight to handle and seldom a danger

the wires selecting them by touch rather than appearance. Hence I am particularly careful about handling and gentling ferret kittens and I find it well worth my while taking time to encourage the kittens to regard my hands as objects bearing gifts rather than hostile appendages that will engender hurt to the ferret. I handle kittens daily and offer them tiny quantities of milk from the palms of my hand. Thus the ferret kittens come to regard my hands as objects which bring pleasure and if I spend ten minutes a day gentling them and giving them tiny quantities of milk it is time well spent. Old time warreners were wont to spit in the palms of their hands and offer the ferret a tiny dab of spittle to drink – a habit that sounds unpleasant to the town-orientated non-ferret keeper but served to encourage the ferret to associate the appearance of the fer-reter's hands with pleasure, for curiously ferrets will drink human saliva with relish.

Thus having reared one's ferrets, gentled them and accustomed them to associate the appearance of the ferreter with a sensation of pleasure it is time to consider training, or perhaps entering is a more correct word, the ferret to quarry.

7

Entering to Quarry

Before attempting to describe the work a ferret is required to perform, it is expedient to determine as to why the ferret performs the task it does. A spaniel may well quest to flush game, to freeze to immobility when the game is flushed, only to retrieve the game to hand, its only reward being the praise of its owner. A ferret manifests no such desire to please and simply creeps to ground, locates its rabbit and attempts to kill it. The fact that the ferret may startle the rabbit into bolting thereby entrapping itself in the nets is both incidental and accidental, for the ferret attacks the rabbit and tries to kill the creature, possibly to eat a morsel of the flesh, but primarily to satiate its desire to kill the rabbit. Ferrets simply do not attempt to deliberately bolt the rabbit, thus qualities such as inefficiency (or inability) in respect to dispatching the rabbit which would render a wild polecat extinct make a ferret particularly valuable. Few people wish for an animal that flashes to ground, grabbing its prey and promptly killing it, and thereby not only preventing the rabbit from bolting but necessitating an often lengthy dig to recover both ferret and rabbit. A ferret that invariably kills its rabbit is certainly not desirable, though sooner or later even the smallest and least aggressive ferret will sometimes kill its prey.

During the golden days of the warrener, at a time when wild rabbits were found commercially in large enclosed warrens, it was customary to muzzle, cope or trim ferrets to prevent them killing the rabbits below ground. Muzzles made of leather or string were often fastened tightly around the ferret's head to prevent the animal opening its mouth, and the ferret released into the warren and invited to do its worst, so to speak. Other variations of the ferret muzzle were the bit muzzle a circular ring of metal through which was fitted a bit that, by dint of a screw thread fitted through the muzzle, tightened the device and also prevented the ferret using its mouth to good advantage. A yet more barbaric method of preventing the ferret opening its jaws was to

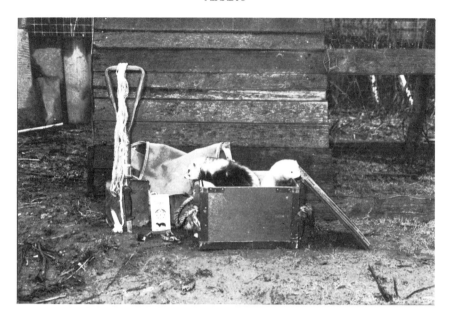

Ferreting kit

Double carrying box

puncture a series of holes (with a hot bradawl) through the lips of the ferret and to weave a length of fine catgut through the said holes. It would be hard to imagine a more barbaric method of muzzling though to puncture a series of holes through the lips of a ferret requires a skill that would put the combined skills of a juggler and a surgeon to shame. The stench emitted by a ferret that was being coped by this method would have rendered the torturer permanently musky and the ferret permanently disturbed. Only twice in my life have I witnessed this atrocity taking place and the stench, screaming and cursing that accompanied the activity has rendered the image of the torture indelibly imprinted in my mind. Frankly it speaks highly of the ferret's disposition that it allows such outrages and still comes readily to hand to be worked.

Equally as injurious, and only slightly less agonising, is the process of snapping off the eye teeth of the ferret with small pliers – an operation that ensures that while the ferret might attack its prey with its tiny incisors it is unable to deliver the death dealing bite (for which ferrets are famous) with its needle sharp carnassial teeth. This process, unlike muzzling and coping, is permanent and not only prevents the ferret from killing, but also impairs the ferret's ability to tear up the meat that should constitute its natural diet. Ferrets subjected to this type of dentistry experience great pain when the vestiges of the carnassial teeth decay and abcesses form at the roots of the coped teeth. Of all the methods so described, snapping off the teeth of the ferret seems to be the most permanently injurious to the ferret though it must be rivalled by the macabre system of threading catgut through lips that have been punctured by a heated bradawl. It is highly unlikely that anyone, other than someone who is mentally disturbed, would consider practising either atrocity in this more enlightened modern age.

In theory the muzzled ferret, or the ferret with its eye teeth removed will actively seek out the rabbit and attempt to kill it if the rabbit fails to bolt. However as the ferret is unable to open its jaws, or in the case of the ferret with its teeth surgically severed, unable to inflict a killing bite, the ferret must resort to scratching at the rump of the rabbit to force it to bolt. This delays the ferret and frustrates the creatures attempt to kill its prey. This, in turn, allows the rabbit to bolt or keeps the ferret so occupied with the bottled up rabbit that the ferreter can, by dint of ingenious devices to be discussed later, detect and dig to the ferret and its undamaged prey. In theory at least the notion is logical, but a coped or muzzled ferret becomes desperately frustrated when muzzled and may react in a disturbed fashion once its muzzle is removed.

What is more terrifying however is the fact that once a rabbit burrow becomes extensive and established it acts as a haven for many other

Two types of carrying box

Setting nets is something of an art

types of animal. Cats, foxes, badgers move into the burrows, excavate them, modify them a little and these areas of the burrow are promptly deserted by rabbits, but these rabbits may still use the entrance passages to the main burrow. When burrows are excavated on rubbish piles, and such places are so well-drained as to provide ideal nesting areas for the rabbits, rats may also take up residence in these burrows. These rats may well eat the odd rabbit kitten or so and will devour the carcasses of rabbit kittens and dead adults alike, but seldom cause enough of a problem for the rabbits to desert the burrow. Ferrets often bolt rats from these burrows, rats ranging from tiny grey rats that easily pass through the meshes of a net to rats half the size of a rabbit, that tangle in the meshes of the net and bite like furies when the ferreter tries to extricate the rat from the nets. Most rats will bolt before a ferret – even a muzzled ferret, and seldom offer a muzzled or coped ferret a serious battle. Yet ferrets are so courageous that, muzzled or coped, the ferret will take the battle to the rat. However, should a ferret bottle up a rat in one of the blind-ended stops that pepper a warren, and should that rat decide to fight, a muzzled or coped ferret has little chance of defending itself yet will be brave enough, or perhaps foolhardy enough, to stand its ground against a rat. Rats bite furiously and fast and the damage a rat can inflict on a muzzled or coped ferret defies belief. I saw coped ferrets worked when I was a child and many times saw ferrets with eyes torn from the sockets and ferrets with muzzles slashed almost in two after they encountered rats in rabbit warrens. Since that time I have never used muzzles of any sort and I advise young ferreters never to use them

A ferret is deemed ready to work to rabbit only when the ferret is fully grown. To work very young ferrets, kits straight from the nest, is bad management and late bred kittens, kittens too small to work at the first frosts, would be best kept until after Christmas until they are entered. It has been argued that wild polecat kittens would need to be able to catch and kill rabbits long before polecats were fully grown, but such an argument is, to say the least, slightly ludicrous. Polecat kittens stay with their dams until the jill finds their presence intolerable or, and this is usually the case, where the litter is an early bred one, the jill becomes sexually ready to accept the male again. Kittens produced in the early months of the year would probably feed on nesting birds, small rodents and tiny rabbits (rabbit kittens still in the nest), and would probably fight shy of tackling adult rabbits. It is also a fact that these days at least many young and mature polecats alike rely quite heavily on road casualty animals and birds to supplement their diets, and when feeding on such meat become road casualties themselves. If true wild polecats (and not fitch-coloured ferrets) still exist in Britain, it is likely that

Llandrindod Wells and parts of Sutherland would host a population. The cadavers of wild polecats (and those of the equally rare pine martens) are often found on the A9 north of Inverness and these corpses are seldom far from the bodies of road casualty rabbits and gulls.

Further evidence of the wisdom of leaving the ferret kittens to mature before working them would emerge if one compared the lot of a wild polecat kitten and a ferret of a similar age. Lorenz suggests that no predator pursues a prey species that is likely to retaliate ferociously or seriously over-tax the efforts of the attacker. A predator, permanently bruised and battered, would soon be rendered *hors de combat* and a suitable candidate for extinction. A young polecat is certainly able to kill a rabbit but will feed on its kill for three days or so before it deems the meat too high to entertain. A young ferret kitten is allowed no such chance of respite and may be required to flush or kill twenty or so rabbits during a single day's work. Thus a ferret kitten worked before it is fully grown, and has attained some of its adult strength, is sorely overtaxed by a ferreting fray at rabbits.

Ferreters are seldom aware of the terrific struggles that sometime take place during the period of time that elapses between the moment the ferret makes contact with the rabbit and the time when the rabbit bolts, or is killed by, the ferret. The furious thumping sound that usually precedes the bolting of the rabbit is usually interpreted as the rabbit signalling danger to the other denizens of the burrow. In fact, the same sound is emitted when a rabbit beset by a ferret endeavours to shake off its attacker, and the efforts of a frightened rabbit can be very bruising to a dog, ferret or a human being who reaches into a hole to extract a live rabbit. Young, immature ferrets are simply not strong enough to endure such treatment and while it is uncommon to find a ferret so badly demoralised that it will refuse to enter a rabbit burrow ever again, there is little doubt that an immature kit which endures harsh treatment from a rabbit may become less efficient as a rabbit hunter because of its premature entering.

Only twice have I found a ferret that was hesitant about tackling rabbits and both times I believe the fault lay in the fact that the ferret had been entered prematurely and had been badly kicked or hurt by the struggles of the rabbit. One ferret, a white jill owned by Peter Beddows of Fradley, Lichfield, lived to thirteen years of age and not only did the jill never kill its rabbit, but the ferret was never found to have fur on its fore paws when it emerged from a burrow after an encounter with a rabbit (this peculiarity will be explained presently). The jill worked until shortly before her death in 1983 and was never known to bite a rabbit. She had been purchased from a livestock market by a would-be ferreter, entered far too young and given to Beddows because of her disinclination to work. She was laid up for a season and entered as a yearling but I believe that despite the fact her hunting instinct compelled her to seek out rabbits her early misadventures detered her from tackling them.

The second tale is a little less pleasant. In 1989 I became in need of new ferrets when I lost my entire crop of seasoned working ferrets. Subsequently I purchased an adult jill that had known a score of homes before I came by her and had developed a set of vices the like of which I have seldom encountered. She sulked if upset, worked only fairly well and had a tendency to lie up at the mouth of a burrow peering out at me, but retreating before my hand when I endeavoured to reach for her. She bottled up rabbits fairly well and towards the end of her first season with me I fitted her with a locator collar and worked her in Strathy, Sutherland. She stayed to ground for quite a time and eventually I was forced to dig to recover her. I broke through to her fairly quickly, for the soil was sandy and the dig relatively easy. I found her rabbit bottled up in a stop and the ferret a foot away from the coney staring hard at the rump of the rabbit, but refraining from attacking it. I reached in, caught up the rabbit dispatched it quickly and then reached for the ferret. To my amazement instead of sliding back into the tunnel as I expected her to do she rushed at my hands and inflicted a series of bites on my hand screaming with fury as she did so.

I was perplexed by the incident but not unduly so, for I felt that digging to her, the sudden appearance of sunlight had startled her and she had attacked me because she had been frightened. However, she repeated the self same performance so often I realised that either I had bought an innately emotionally disturbed ferret or that some incident in her life had produced these undesirable characteristics. Perhaps her frequent changes of ownership had unnerved her, but I have known many ferrets that have been swopped and changed repeatedly but did not behave in such a manner. So bizarre was her behaviour that I became curious and traced her history to the time she had come from Norfolk to Caithness as a kitten. She had been purchased in mid-August by one of the now settled ex-itinerant children that have been rehomed on one of the council estates in Wick and worked to rabbit within hours of her arrival. I would hazard a guess that her first days in Caithness had been traumatic. She had been worked too young and henceforth she had behaved erratically when she encountered rabbits. To end the tale on a somewhat higher note, when the season ended I mated her to another white ferret, bred an entirely satisfactory litter from her and rehomed the jill as a pet.

Many of the sporting books and articles published during Victorian and Edwardian times would have one believe that there were arcane scents known only to naturalists and warreners concerned with the process of entering young ferrets – but this is quite absurd. It is equally absurd to suggest that before ferrets were taken into the field they should be subjected to a training programme allowing them to run through pipes and tubes to accustom them to exploring the ramifications of a rabbit warren. The mustelids from weasels to wolverines have an insatiable curiosity concerning holes and dark passages and literally seek to explore any crevice they encounter. A ferret will seek to explore folds in the carpet or up trouser legs to satiate this curiosity and trappers since time immemorial have exploited the inquisitive nature of mustelids by placing traps of various kinds in pipes and artificial tunnels which mustelids usually find irresistable places to explore. Hence a ferret will need little preliminary training before it is taken on its first hunting trip.

It is however good policy to accustom a youngster to being boxed or bagged prior to being taken hunting and a few spells of incarceration in the ferret box do little harm and serve to produce a ferret that is not disturbed by being transported. This, and this alone, is the only training a kitten needs before it is taken hunting and newcomers to the world of ferreting would do well to ignore advice on how a ferret needs to be conditioned and trained prior to it being taken out on its first hunting trip.

On reaching a set of burrows the ferreter believes to be occupied, the ferreter should lift the lid of the carrying box and allow the ferret to get accustomed to the sunlight. When the ferret has grown accustomed to the bright light it should be placed in the mouth of the rabbit burrow and allowed to exercise its instincts. The ferret will usually sniff around the perimeter of the entrance and then, as if led by some invisible leash, it will creep into the burrow slowly exploring the myriad scents that come wafting up from the bowels of the burrow. Some young kits seem to know instinctively that, as Conan Doyle would say, 'the game's afoot' and indicate the presence of a rabbit with a shake of the tail or with the hairs of the tail raised in a bottle brush fashion. Some ferreters advise starving the kitten prior to its first hunting trip, but this is both unnecessary and decidedly counter-productive. Ferrets hunt because they are compelled to hunt. They seek out the scents of prey creatures because they enjoy seeking out these scents and it is totally unnecessary to starve a ferret to stimulate the hunting instinct. A young kitten should be well fed before it is taken out on its first trip, and strong enough and fit enough to handle a strongly kicking rabbit.

Yet imperative as the hunting instinct is, a young ferret may well fail

It is essential to clear cover before setting nets

to find a rabbit on its first hunting trip despite the fact that the burrow into which the ferret has been inserted is quite obviously a small burrow. The fact is that an apparently short burrow will seldom consist of a single tube joining entrance to single exit for short tunnels called 'stops', blind ended tunnels into which rabbits creep to sleep or sometimes to nest, lead off from the main tunnels. An inexperienced ferret may well fail to find a rabbit that is lying up in one of these 'stops'. I invariably choose one of these short burrows to start a ferret and seldom put a ferret to ground in a burrow a dog has failed to mark or declare 'inhabited' (the subject of marking dogs and dogs employed to work with ferrets will be dealt with presently). Yet I have known many young ferrets fail to find in a warren that is patently occupied by rabbits.

A tale will easily illustrate a point. Living as I do in an area that is sparsely populated with people, rearing litters of ferrets is not good practice. Yet it is often expedient to mate jills to prevent the myriad disorders that attend unmated female ferrets. Thus I often put out pregnant jills to friends who enjoy rearing ferret kittens and have a market for these young ferrets. In autumn I bring home my jills, together with an odd ferret kitten, to train on to replace elderly ferrets I am considering retiring. A young hob returned to me with the adult jill, and because he was both active and well grown, I entered him within days of his arrival. My lurcher bitch Merab marked a very short burrow scarcely a few yards in length, and behaved so excitedly that it was obvious that the burrow held a rabbit. I placed the young hob at the mouth of the warren and his tail bottled brushed as he scented the rabbit. However the hob bustled through the burrow to emerge seconds later at the exit to the burrow. Merab continued to mark at the entrance however. I replaced the hob at the entrance to the burrow, and once more the ferret simply walked through the burrow and emerged with a slightly cross expression on its face. However to write off a young ferret after a single trip is lunacy and as the day progressed the hob bolted a number of rabbits. At the close of the day I returned to the burrow in which the ferret had failed to find. The hob sniffed its way into the depths of the burrow and seconds later a rabbit bolted, the hob hot on its heels. It is wise to remember that even mature seasoned ferrets often fail to find in large burrows with a great number of stops leading off the main tunnels. Hence it is good sense not to be too ambitious when starting a youngster and to start the youngster in a recently established burrow that is not too extensive.

Careful handling and careful management of the working ferret during the early stages of its education is always advisable if the young kitten is to grow into a competent and efficient mature worker. If the young kitten chances on its rabbit, bottles it up and refuses to leave its catch the ferreter will sometimes need to dig to the kitten. A bad experience at the end of a dig, earth falling in on the kitten, the ferret accidentally struck with a spade etc. is very detrimental to the development of the ferret. Many of the faults and foibles manifested by mature ferrets offered for sale by disenchanted field sportsmen have been generated during the time when the young kitten was in the process of being entered. With careful and sensible entering a young kitten will develop few foibles and fewer faults.

The most upsetting experience that can beset a young ferret just starting out on its career can occur if the young ferret encounters a dog that is antipathetic to ferrets. A ferret, excited or elated by its first encounter with a rabbit, emerging to find a hostile dog lunging and chopping at it can be permanently ruined. I suspect many of the skulkers, ferrets that hang about in the mouths of burrows just out of reach of the ferreters hands, have developed such a fault because the ferreter has snatched them up roughly when they emerged from their first engagement with a rabbit or worse still the ferret has met with a hostile dog during its early training days. It is lunacy to take out any ferret alongside a dog which might attack it, and lunacy twice over to enter a young kit when such a dog is present.

A few years ago I forsook an excellent rabbiting estate because the associate nominated to hunt rabbit on the estate insisted on bringing along his chocolate-coloured Dobermann on our ferreting trips. Why he took along this ill mannered brute is a mystery, for the dog seldom chased, let alone caught, a rabbit but was incredibly hostile to ferrets. My associate made no effort to restrain the dog, and if a ferret lay up my associate would wander off, gun in hand, to seek out crows and rooks while his dog gazed menacingly down the hole he had observed the ferret disappear. I was never a brave man, but many times I set about the hulk to prevent it from killing my ferrets and eventually I saw so many useful ferrets changed into skulkers by associating with this lop-eared menace that I broke with its owner. I lost track of the Dobermann-owning gun man until in 1987 I read of a horrendous case of a woman driven demented by the behaviour of her husband and had killed him with a meat cleaver. There was something so familiar about the face of the accused that I read the article concerning the murder and quite suddenly in my mind's eye I saw, not a murder victim, but a chocolate-coloured Dobermann gazing down a rabbit warren. Only later in the day did my mind connect the relationship between the victim and the vision of the Dobermann.

The first few trips to the hunting field make or break the ferret, or can render a kitten a priceless worker or a useless brute that can ruin a day's hunting and infuriate the owner so much that he cares little as to whether or not the ferret is lost. True I still breed the occasional, slightly less than useful, ferret. I own a very unreliable hob at the time of writing, but I seldom breed a ferret that is sulky, vicious or, worst of all, a skulker who lies in the mouth of a burrow for an inordinately lengthy period of time and can often spoil an otherwise excellent day's ferreting. Innately vicious ferrets must occasionally be born, nervy edgy animals with habits akin to those of wild polecats but the majority of 'strange' ferrets are ruined by bad or erratic handling early in the career of the kitten. A young ferret that has just engaged and bolted a rabbit will usually emerge from the bolt hole fairly soon after the appearance of the rabbit, heated by the contest and usually fairly edgy. A kitten emerging in such a manner may well stop at the mouth of the burrow and gaze around a moment before leaving the exit. To snatch at a young ferret when it stops to investigate the outside world after it has observed a rabbit flash out of the said burrow is bad management practice. A ferret should be allowed to emerge from the burrow before it is picked up boxed or inserted into another hole. A ferret that is snatched up repeatedly will usually retreat into the warren to escape capture as soon as it observes a hand reaching for it. The skulker, the most irritating of hunting auxilliaries, the most maddening of all kinds of ferret, is born from habits such as these.

A young ferret emerging from a conflict with a rabbit, or worse still a rat, is often so excited by the conflict that it will sometimes bite the hand that reaches for it. I make it a point to allow the ferret to settle and compose itself before reaching for it and boxing it and I have seen unpleasant accidents occur when this advice is not heeded. When I ratted and rabbited at Swinton, Yorkshire, I watched a pale sandy hob owned by a friend of mine bite with great fury when the ferret which emerged tail in a gale hot on the heels of a bolting rabbit was snatched up to be boxed. The hob had been engaged in a furious battle with the rabbit it had bolted and had emerged after a half hour stint of attempting to bolt the rabbit and had been temporarily blinded by the sunlight. I assume it had believed the hand of my friend to be the rabbit returning to the battle and had bitten furiously when it had been touched. The hob was ordinarily as tame as a kitten and would not have attempted to bite if it had been allowed time to accustom its eyes to the sunlight and time to allow its excitement to wane a little. As it was, my friend seldom gave the hob time to settle so the hob reacted accordingly!

The rabbit, unlike the hare, enjoys no legal protection during its breeding season – it is illegal to sell or expose for sale any hare or leveret between the months of March and July inclusive – but it is an extremely short-sighted policy to ferret for rabbits during the breeding season. Does are then milky and it is not to everyones liking to eat suckling animals and rabbit kittens, naked and helpless in the nest, fall easy victims to a ferret. A ferret worked in mid-summer is sure to kill and eat kittens that are unable to bolt before it and hence a days ferreting in warm weather assumes an aura of futility.

Living as I do in the extreme north of Scotland, in a country where extremely cold winter temperatures delay the rabbit's breeding cycle, I usually continue ferreting until mid-March though a warm spell that induces doe rabbits to come into season and produce young always brings my season's hunting to an end. Such spells of warm weather are rare at these latitudes and hence I continue ferreting until I observe buck scud, fur torn from fighting buck rabbits – near to the breeding burrows. This is a sure sign that the does are in season, or in kindle, and I cease ferreting forthwith.

I resume hunting as soon as the first frosts of autumn cause the undergrowth near the burrows to shed its leaves. Along the coastal fringes, in dry valleys near cliff faces, rabbits commonly nest in lairs that are protected by stunted dog rose bushes and I regard the shedding of the leaves of these bushes as a sign that the rabbits have ceased breeding for the season. I have been misled by these signs only twice, once in mid-winter 1987 when a mild mid-winter spell caused does to mate and conceive and again in 1990 when, in the depths of mid-winter, I bolted and netted a very pregnant doe rabbit. I hasten to add that when I netted the doe and realised my mistake I released the pregnant doe in the hopes that the trauma of being caught had not damaged the litter.

A rabbit hunter should in fact avoid an extermination programme, catching and killing all the rabbits living in a certain pocket of land, but treat the wildlife of the area with some respect, pruning rather than felling so to speak. The rabbit is so prolific, so fecund that it can, and will, survive a furious culling programme providing a few rabbits are left to perpetuate the species. Rabbits breed rapidly and the fecundity of a rabbit has long inspired naturalists with a penchant for geometrical progressions to calculate the number of progeny and descendants a pair of rabbits could produce in a given period of time. Thomas Bewick in his book *A Natural History of British Quadrupeds* (1814) suggests that a rabbit might, in a good season, breed some seven times a year producing eight young in each litter. He calculates that such a doe might produce 1,274,840 descendants in a four year period. Copeland, *Agriculture, Ancient and Modern* (1866), believes that eight litters would not be taxing the doe unduly and calculates that in four years the doe would have 2,164,800 descendants to her credit. A single pair of rabbits left on an area that has been subject to a drastic culling programme will in a good season produce fifty to sixty kittens, but the mortality rate is far higher than either Bewick or Copeland envisaged. Cats, dogs, foxes, stoats, weasels and rats slay the kittens with alacrity while buzzards and crows also take their toll on the unwary kittens. Thus to leave a single pair of rabbits in a previously heavily infested rabbit colony is not good management and the hunter may well expect a bad season's hunting the year following such a cull.

Myxomatosis however can have a far more damaging effect on the rabbit population than even a drastic cull. This disease inflicts heavy losses on our local rabbit population during mid- to late-August until the end of the breeding season and for this reason local rabbit catchers, or pest control officers, who sell rabbit carcasses rather than simply poisoning rabbits, start a cull in the early days of August, despite the fact that does are still in kindle at this time. Personally, I leave a badly infested area for a season after I observe the disease has taken a heavy toll on the rabbit population. Burrows, the inhabitants of which have been wiped out by the disease, usually fall in and appear less than attractive to rabbits seeking to re-populate an infected area and many of the survivors of the disease will resort to nesting in deep cover rather than returning to infected warrens. The mortality rate of kittens reared in such conditions is usually much higher than amongst kittens reared in established burrows. Hence an area recovering from the effects of a particularly virulent form of myxomatosis may take longer to restock itself with rabbits than would the same area if the rabbits had been almost exterminated by a particularly savage cull.

So let us assume one has entered the ferret and that the kitten, which has not been subjected to stresses, problems or bad handling, has matured into a fine working, albeit immature, young ferret. How now does one go about catching the rabbits the ferret has bolted. Basically rabbits bolted from a warren might be caught by:

a. Catching the rabbits in purse nets.
b. Entrapping the rabbits in a long net that has been set to encircle the warren.
c. Allowing dogs to chase and catch the rabbits.
d. Shooting the rabbits as they bolt.
e. Hawking the bolted rabbits.

8

Nets

Bateman, *Animal Traps and Trapping* (1971), attributes man's success in the colonisation and subjugation of the planet to his ability to imitate and improve on the devices used by other species. The Venus Flytrap almost exactly resembles the jaws of the gin trap, and snares were simply man's adaptation of the coils of vines and lianas that, from time to time, entrap mammals, reptiles and birds in their sinuous creepers. If Bateman is correct, then there seems little doubt that man copied and improved on the sundry web-like structures used by certain species of spider and produced nets, namely the long nets and the purse nets, of the ferreter and fox hunter.

Basically, purse nets are nets that are laid out to cover the bolt holes of a rabbit in such a manner that, should a rabbit enmesh itself, the net will close around its victim – pursing until the rabbit's chance of escaping becomes minimal. These nets are made of either nylon or hemp – and nylon nets are virtually rot-proof and so resistant to the elements that the net ring will often corrode long before the nylon fabric of the net decays. Nylon nets are produced on net knitting machines and hence are very cheap to purchase. On the debit side such nets are prone to tangle if not handled carefully and it can be very tedious work untangling unkempt nets. I must confess that I stopped using nylon nets after a godson, confident and sure of his ability as only the very young can be, borrowed my nets after assuring me that he knew all about ferreting! The nets were returned in such a tangle that I spent many of my break times at the school where I was teaching at the time unravelling the muddle. I gave the youth the untangled nets and bought in hemp nets only to find the boy had lost interest in field sports and discovered girls. My nets probably reside to this day at the bottom of his wardrobe.

Hemp nets are hand made, for the fibrous nature of hemp clogs machines that are used for net making. The disadvantages of hemp are

Part and parcel of every serious ferreter's kit

many. Firstly the material is made from a natural product and hence, like all vegetable products, subject to decay. Secondly, brand new nets, or untreated new nets (and I shall deal with the subject of preservatives presently), are prone to run badly when a rabbit strikes them and this will sometimes allow the rabbit to escape. This is a trifling matter, for the ferreter can simply hang the nets by the pegs and punch the purse with his fists to imitate the action of a rabbit striking the nets. The tiny hemp fibres that will sometimes prevent the net running as freely as it might are thus broken and the nets hereafter will run true and entrap the rabbit. Hemp nets often tangle during the first times they are put to use, but this problem too is resolved once the nets have been used a few times and the tiny hemp fibres that cause a net to tangle broken free.

Hemp nets are expensive and justify the few pence extra it costs to preserve them. I invariably soak my nets in a bath of wood preservative, a green creosote-based liquid I bought at my local saw mills, leave the nets a further month to dry out and only then do I consider using them. The nets are often sticky after such treatment but dry out and seldom tangle for the hemp fibres are now forced to adhere to the main strand of the net by the adhesive action of the preservative. I had some proof of the efficacy of this treatment in 1989 when a band of young men visited me in Caithness, borrowed both my nets and ferrets and proceeded to 'work' a bleak windswept coastline to the north of Sutherland. My ferrets were returned unscathed as were my nets – well at least some of them – but when I returned to the coastline a full year later after a winter of snow, ice and freezing conditions, I found eleven of my nets still covering bolt holes, unchanged, unrotted and undamaged by a year in the open air. I still work these nets to this day I must add, though the rings suffered a shade through their contact with the salt air of the Sutherland coast.

On the subject of making nets it is expedient that I should say as little as possible. I have made many nets – under the supervision of others more competent than I, but once left to my own devices my nets become a fearsome tangle of strands of hemp, skillessly clinging to other lengths of hemp twine. After a while I accepted the truth that I was one of the most mechanically inept of people and bought in my nets. Later I was to make an arrangement with the Jackson family, a group of extremely adept net makers, to give them a lurcher puppy every sixteen years or so in exchange for all the nets I needed. I am extremely inept at net making, but I am able to make deals that favour me!

So the nets one is able to buy: now to the setting of those nets to entrap rabbits bolted by the ferrets. Each net is surrounded by a small cord called a draw line and the loose ends of the draw line should be affixed to a wooden or steel peg. This peg is fastened in the soil atop of the bolt hole and the net spread across and around the hole, so that the action of the rabbit striking the net will cause the net to purse and entrap the rabbit. Certain holes, particularly holes in mature warrens will need either two nets or skillful manipulation of nets by the ferreter to cover the warrens. In fact it is fair to say that, unless a ferreter has access to a large area of land that is thickly populated with rabbits, it will take several years for the ferreter to become competent at the task or skill of setting nets in curious places. I served my apprenticeship by setting nets to entrap rabbits that were feeding on refuse tips near Rotherham and I learned to place nets over bolt holes amongst corroded refrigerators or washing machines. Hence I like nets that are somewhat larger than conventional nets for it is easier to cover curious-shaped bolt holes with a large net than with the smaller more usual two foot six inch nets. Many ferreters, net makers far more skilful than I am, will often knit very large nets to cover a series of bolt holes that are not only adjacent to each other, but so close as to make covering with several conventional-sized nets impractical.

Some net makers will deliberately colour nets to make them inconspicuous, but this is a questionable practice by any standards. Rabbits are probably colour-blind – they do not have the types of rod and cone structures that are found in human eyes or in the eyes of other mammals that are probably able to determine colour. Human beings are, however, able to determine colour, but find the collection of carefully camouflaged nets set amongst greenery or brambles difficult. Certainly I find more green nets that have been left behind by ferreters than I find undyed nets. Frankly, undyed hemp nets are difficult enough to recover, particularly amongst bramble patches, without adding further camouflaging. Camouflaged nets probably do not confuse rabbits, but certainly confuse human beings.

Antique warrens, ancient, well-used burrows the surface of the runs to which has long since erroded the floor of the entrances to the burrows, can often be the very devil to net. Mouths of such burrows have often fallen in to reveal a single hole that is not only too large to net but concealing three of four holes leading from the mouth of the burrow. These burrows need careful netting or, if they cannot be netted, need blocking with turf, stones or branches of wood.

Perhaps at this point it would be wise to discuss not only the structure of rabbit burrows but how the ferreter might determine as to whether such burrows are inhabited or not. Single hole burrows are seldom as straight forward as they may first appear and a simple passage into the depths of the burrow may well divide into many tunnels the ramifications of which are sometimes immense. At the time of writing I often ferret a bank of soil adjacent to some pine trees in Dornoch, Sutherland, and one of these burrows in this bank is a single-holed affair that is so extensive that I have yet to be able to bolt a rabbit from its depths. I have followed the progress of a ferret with a locator in this particular burrow and the bleeper indicates that the burrow stretches for nearly an acre and attains a depth of nearly eight feet in areas near the pine trees where the roots of the pines have provided good drainage and easy digging. It is certainly not the easiest place to ferret and I have decided to leave the denizens of the said burrow in peace.

I shall not dwell on the habits of the rabbit, or the structure of the burrows in which rabbits live for, I have dwelt on this subject at considerable length in my book In Pursuit of Coney. Sufficient to say that a typical burrow has many blind-ended passages known as 'stops' leading from the central passage and when a rabbit decides not to bolt, or finds itself trapped by the ferret, it will seek out the sanctuary of such a stop (and I shall explain the expression 'sanctuary' presently) and sit head into the stop, haunches filling the tunnel as tightly as a cork in a bottle. A ferret encountering such a rabbit will often scratch at the rump of the rabbit, sometimes furiously denuding the rump of fur in an attempt to creep over the back of the coney to bite at the head or neck of the rabbit. If a rabbit is prepared to sit out the fury of the ferret, the ferret will often tire of its efforts and leave the rabbit to survive until another day. In country where wild polecats or feral ferrets are found, rabbits with their haunches almost scraped to the flesh are sometimes taken by trappers and lampers. Some ferrets are particularly vigorous in attacking the rumps of rabbits bottled up in stops and these are prized by many ferreters for being 'good stayers', ferrets that will stick with the rabbit long enough for the ferreter to dig to them. Other ferrets will take little interest in the rump of the rabbit and will often leave the burrow or change rabbits if a coney adopts this defensive posture.

I am of the opinion that much of the noise that occurs when a ferret is put to ground in a burrow – the thumping, the banging etc. – emanates from the conflict between the rabbit and the ferret, for some rabbits kick vigorously to prevent the ferret clambering over their backs to dispatch the coney with a neck or head bite. This kicking action can be particularly wounding as anyone who has been kicked by a bottled up rabbit can attest, and many times I have seen young ferrets bested by robust strong rabbits. Anyone who has dug to a stopped up rabbit is also able to state how firmly the coney can wedge itself in the stop, for it requires a particularly strenuous effort on the part of the ferreter to pull some unharmed rabbits from such places.

Not all nets will hold bolted rabbits, no matter how skillfully the ferreter places them, and the tyro ferreter would do well to treat tales of other ferreters whose nets always hold bolters with a grain of salt. Some rabbits will strike the nets at odd angles pushing the meshes aside without causing the nets to purse. Others will throw the nets with their heads without becoming enmeshed in the strands. Other rabbits strike the nets with such force that the pegs are pulled from the earth leaving the rabbit bound in the net to race off to seek sanctuary. Usually as such rabbits struggle, run or hop the meshes of the nets tangle yet further and prevent the progress of the rabbit, but this is not always the case. In 1986 I spent my first season in the Highlands, ferreting in Sutherland and twice I bolted rabbits that were alive, fairly active yet encased in nets, one of which bore the mark of antiquity. The life of a rabbit impeded with such a device must be fairly horrific yet both rabbits were of average weight and size and still had reserves of body fat. I have several times caught rabbits with both pieces of net and snares attached to their bodies, necks and legs and once found a rabbit with a fragment of net entwined around a hind leg the tissue of which was necrotic. It speaks highly of the tenacity of the coney that it can survive such accidents and injuries. Yet any netter worthy of the name of field sportsman would seek out any injured or netted escapee rabbit and dispatch

A properly set net

The ferret comes to investigate the netted entrance

the animal rather than let the creature suffer from both its attachments and its afflictions.

Rabbits should be dispatched while still enmeshed in the nets and not after they have been unravelled and examined. The ferreter should always do his best not to cause unnecessary terror, cruelty or pain to the rabbits that he hunts and to delay the dispatching of a rabbit for any reason is blatant cruelty. I have several times noticed the terror rabbits experience when a ferreter has carefully unravelled the nets from the rabbit prior to killing the creature. This display of histrionics serves no useful purpose, though it may well look impressive to some. A live, strong healthy rabbit is quite difficult to extricate from the nets as it will often kick violently and sometimes bite. A dead rabbit offers no such resistance.

If the ferreter works unusual spots he must expect to find not only rabbits caught up in his nets. A tale with a slight Munchausen flavour about it was related by a friend of mine who ferreted some burrows on the Lincolnshire/Norfolk border. Nets were set, but a lurcher wandering from the ferreting party (scarcely good management one should add), ran a green but large leveret hard in the field adjoining the ferreting party. When the hare was hard pressed it flashed back into the field where the group was engaged in ferreting and raced down a rabbit warren only to be netted up or back-netted as one would say in ferreting parlance.

Cats, both feral and, in the extreme north of Britain, bonafide wild-cats Felis sylvestris grampensis will often lie up in rabbit warrens and strange as it may seem readily bolt if a ferret pesters them. These cats, both wild and feral, become both frightened and furious when entangled in the nets and in seconds net and cat become inextricably tangled. To extract a cat from such a tangle is a terrifying task for a frightened cat will cause damage that is apparently out of proportion to its size and appearance. At one time I tried to extract cats from these tangles and received terrible maulings as a result of my efforts. Now I cut both losses and nets to release the cats. I find it safer and less distressing to both myself and the occupants of the nets.

Foxes too bolt readily before a ferret, providing that is the fox has not been driven in, or is aware of, the ferreting party. When a frightened fox encounters a ferret the outcome of the engagement is obviously a very dead ferret. Lucas records in his *Hunt and Working Terriers* that at one time McNeill, then Master of the Grafton Foxhounds, worked with the North Cotswold in country that was heavily infested with rabbits and when the foxes used quite small rabbit burrows to den, McNeill disdained the use of terriers to bolt foxes but relied on the use of a large buck (hob) ferret. Foxes are sometimes entrapped in rabbit nets but unless the net is large and firmly pegged the fox will bolt carrying the net with him to throw off the meshes at its leisure. In 1981 I worked a large, but not a particularly productive, rabbiting country in Leicester and bolted many foxes. One threw off the meshes only after I pursued the creature for nearly half a mile. My lurchers were at that time fairly timid creatures and disdained from tackling the fox, even though it was incapacitated by nets.

Should a fox become entangled in nets however, and should the net peg hold the fox, it is simplicity itself to release the fox from the meshes. Foxes become catatonic or experience a reaction nearly identical to catatonia when they become entangled and remain glossy eyed, breathing lightly and moving not at all for a few seconds after capture and this will allow the ferreter ample time to release the captive fox. Once released, once allowed to recover, the fox will hightail it away from the ferreter apparently undamaged by what must have been a traumatic experience.

However while rabbiters show a great tolerance of entrapped foxes and cats few experience anything but revulsion when a rat becomes enmeshed in the nets. Most rats will glide through nets with the ease with which a small jill ferret will negotiate the meshes, but not so large and pregnant doe rats. I served my time, so to speak, rabbiting on refuse piles in Rotherham – a particularly productive time sportwise I must add – and where there is suitable food adjacent to rabbit warrens, rats will den up in the burrows. More than once I have been a little too eager to seize a furry bundle that had been entrapped in the nets only to find I had seized a rat. Despite the fact that for some twenty-three halcyon years I ran a rat pack – a band of sometimes sixty terriers and more than once have I live caught rats, I have yet to overcome my sense of revulsion when I have inadvertently seized a netted rat. For hours afterwards my hands feel unclean and the cold sweat that appears on my neck after such a mistake is very slow to dry. I release foxes and will even cut away my nets to free a trapped cat, but I always kill rats that I find enmeshed in my rabbit nets. I am decidedly anthropomorphic where rats are concerned and despite my scientific training I attribute rats with a host of unpleasant social characteristics.

If I might return to the subject of back-netting for a moment or so. I work thickly infested rabbiting country at the northernmost shore of the British mainland, a country that is so grossly overstocked with rabbits that sheep find it difficult to obtain a living from the raised beaches along the shoreline. Few burrows are more than thirty-five yards or so from adjacent burrows and rabbits that escape the nets either by brushing aside the meshes of the nets, or escaping via the unguarded bolt hole, will usually find sanctuary in nearby burrows. Hence, before I place a ferret to ground I net up nearby burrows which will afford safety for the bolting rabbit and drive the net pegs in deeply lest the rabbits strike the nets and take nets and pegs deep into the burrows. When I worked to nets regularly – I no longer net every burrow as I shall explain presently – I caught a great many rabbits by dint of back-netting – a fact that either illustrates how numerous the rabbits are in this neck of the woods or how inept I am at setting nets correctly perhaps!

Despite the fact that I am often remiss at taking my time and setting nets correctly I am loathe to allow strangers to lift and fold my nets once it is patently obvious the ferrets have no further business in a particular burrow. I am also reluctant to lend my nets these days, not so much because such nets may become lost – and they often are I must admit – but simply because when such nets are returned to me they are often so hopelessly tangled that it takes me days to unravel the meshes so that the nets may be used again. Yet if the nets are properly folded they seldom tangle and can be used time and time again without resembling a macrame knot. I lift nets placing my thumbs in the net rings and shake the meshes so that the detritus, strands of grass, thorn and bramble fall from them. I then twine such nets in a figure of eight around my thumb and forefinger finally wrapping the draw line around the figure of eight bundle. Thus packed not only are the nets unable to tangle in the meshes of other nets, but are folded into tight bundles that are easy to pack. At one time, in the unhappy days when most of my nets were made of nylon, I folded my nets some four times before placing them in my net bag but found that by the end of the day they were slightly tangled no matter how carefully I placed them, but the very worst tangle I ever experienced taught me my lesson.

In order to explain what happened involves a confession that may render me a little less than manly in the eyes of the reader. I have an absolute dread of horses, a dread that does not have its genesis in a riding accident, for I have yet to summon up courage enough to back a horse, nor has a horse or anything equine done me physical harm. I am simply afraid of horses. So having revealed a rather pitiful foible it is expedient to get on with my tale. I was ferreting a bank near Blackwell, Derby, a rather swish farm; a well kept, well maintained place that specialised in producing quite rare breeds of cattle and a host of other curious almost extinct breeds of livestock. The land was badly infested with rabbits that had somehow undermined the foundations of a stable and around this very unlikely location I had decided to set my nets. Alas, stables house horses and subsequently it was only a matter of time before I became harassed by a very irate Welsh Cob stallion that not only put my lurchers to flight but caused me to reach for my nets, hastily bag them and race off like the coward I am, so to speak. My fear of the animal unnerved the beast who set off in hot pursuit of me and I fell heavily on a slope straining my back and allowing my net bag to fall free. My stallion – I exaggerate, the beast was not old enough to be called a stallion – my colt promptly attacked the bag striking it with his teeth and kicking the bag around the field pounding the rucksack with its front hooves and raining kicks on the object with his hind legs. I literally sprang over the fence and ran to my hostess, with no shame for my behaviour and the terror I was experiencing, and breathlessly gulped out my tale. She promptly walked into the paddock, slapped the over-frisky youngster, thereby stopping his antics, and fetched out my very dishevelled net bag. I felt mildly ashamed of my cowardice; a cowardice matched only by that of my two lurchers which promptly vanished when danger of any sort threatened, but the sight of my crushed and battered rucksack acted as a balm for my pride. My hostess explained that what the horse was displaying was typical of coltish behaviour and he meant no harm. However it took me nearly a week to untangle the nets within the rucksack but I had ample time to complete the task laid up as I was with a damaged back. Since then I have always balled up my nets as I have described. I would like just for once to relate a tale that has even a machismo twist, but sadly my life is peppered with incidents that reveal my somewhat pathetic shortcomings.

Thus how to fold and pack nets but at the end of the season it is best to unravel and unroll the nets, to clean out any pieces of vegetable matter that cling to the fibres, and hang the nets in a cool dry place for the summer. I feel terribly hypocritical giving such advice for the end of most ferreting seasons finds my nets still rolled and packed in my very battered and muddy net bag. Yet the passage of air around hanging nets does a great deal to prevent the rotting of hemp nets – and such nets are prone to rot despite the fact that I soak them in preservative for a month before I start the season. Properly cared for nets will last a lifetime and in 1966 while living in Rotherham I was given a set of hemp nets that had been made in 1920, had served several seasons and had finally lain idle for ten or so years. They were in excellent condition, virtually undam-aged and still functioned as well as they had done some thirty years previous. To my eternal shame I ill-treated the nets badly and when I left Rotherham to move to Lichfield some two years later the nets were in the same, rather moth eaten, condition my own nets enjoyed. I confess that I am equally cavalier in my treatment of spades, cutting tools, saws and, more recently, locators and while I do not expect to get thirty years service from jute nets I know of several people who are careful enough to obtain a lifetime of service from such equipment.

Nylon nets too benefit from hanging up throughout the summer, though such nets are resistant to bacteria, fungi and the type of insect life that plays the very devil with hemp meshes. The rings attached to nylon nets will often show signs of rusting if the nets are kept rolled and folded inside bags – and lest the reader should believe that the hot spelter dip into which these rings are dipped makes the rings totally impervious to the effect of wind and weather, I suggest that the reader examines nets that have endured a mere week or so of ill treatment by being 'left down' in a region adjacent to the sea. Galvanising, hot spelter treatment will not prevail against the salt air of such districts and most rings begin to show some sign of rust after a mere week in winter weather.

The majority of ferreting books make mention of long nets that can be used to skirt a particularly extensive warren and catch up rabbits that have escaped the meshes of the purse nets. Since 1953 when myxomatosis nearly placed the rabbit on the endangered species list few spots are so overrun with conies as to justify the use of long nets, though in recent years the rabbit has started to overcome the disease by developing a resistance to the virus. I dwelt too long on the subject of myxomatosis in my book *In Pursuit of Coney* to elaborate on the disease in the pages of a book concerned only with ferreting, but the reader is unlikely to be asked to clear an area that is so infested with rabbits as to justify the use of a long net. Long nets are expensive, often quite cumbersome to carry – hemp long nets are particularly heavy one should add – and seldom justify the expense of purchase.

However, let us assume that the reader does have access to complex burrows in a district where rabbits are becoming such a nuisance that they need to be exterminated rather than thinned. In such circumstances the use of a long net might well be justified. However very few ferreters will experience such conditions and so, unless the would-be ferreter has a great deal of ferreting country and a great many rabbits to cull, the long net is superfluous to the needs of the ferreter. At one time Alan Bryant ran a field sport supplies company at Windsor and sold many long nets. He once stated that few of these long nets were unfurled, let alone used, and spent their lives in the same carrier bag that had enclosed them at the time of their purchase.

There is virtually no magic and little expertise in setting up a long net and the reason that long netting has acquired this curious ethos is that there are few places where a long net can be used and few people who attempt to use them. A long net can, with very little practice, be set up with great efficiency and great speed – an associate of mine, Paul Moore of Brighton, sets a hundred yard net in under three minutes even in slightly windy conditions, though his behaviour must seem curious to anyone watching a man unfurl a long net at the speed of a sprint runner.

Long nets can only justify their use if

a. The country is over run with rabbits.
b. The landowner asks for an extermination programme rather than a cull.
c. The burrows are extensive and virtually impossible to cover using purse nets.
d. The burrows are found in deep gorse and are impossible to work with purse nets.

and usually rabbits living in such locations will attempt to hop from gorse patch to gorse patch and not run far enough to be entangled in a long net.

At this juncture perhaps it is expedient to mention that epic in futility – night ferreting – an exercise that seems to serve no useful purpose other than to hunt a section of land where the hunter is unwelcome. Ferrets become easily lost during daylight hours and after dark regularly wander far from the burrows. I have never understood why ferreters adopt this bizarre, inefficient and somewhat pointless exercise on land where they have permission to hunt. At night rabbits are out feeding and while this may result in some rabbits being caught by back-netting, running them back into holes that are covered with purse nets, rabbits that are driven into their holes in order to be ferreted out of the same burrows are only too aware of the dangers that await them should they decide to bolt.

Night ferreting conjures up the image of the night time skulker, the activities of a man who, though he is not to be feared, is seldom to be trusted. I have never enjoyed such an image and it is an image I have taken some pains to avoid acquiring: hence I have never considered night ferreting to be a worthwhile activity. Once, and only once, did I engage in such lunacy for my host rather enjoyed spicing his life with peculiar experiences and requested I accompany him on a foray during the early hours of an October morning. As I hunted the property by daylight I felt obliged to come on the foray but declined to bring either ferrets, nets or dogs. My host brought along his nephew who carried all the equipment that indicated the youth was new to field sports – brand new nets, someone else's cast off ferrets and a net carrier bag straight out of Vogue. To state that the evening was a catastrophe would be an understatement and dawn found us soaked to the skin desperately digging up a huge burrow to recover two rather frightened hob ferrets. The dig continued until twelve noon of the following day for the warren was situated near a cottage, the owner of which kept Khaki Campbell ducks – vittles that would prove irrestible to a wayfaring ferret. At 9.00 a.m. my host had gone home to attend to more important business and at the next fall of icy rain the nephew too found more important things to do and also departed the scene. I dug on, a flush of venomous hate giving energy to my digging, and at 11.30 a.m. recovered the first hob. I crated the hob in a brand new carrying box and sat down on the muddy earth to lament my fate. Just when all seemed hopeless I glanced at the crater I had dug to observe the other hob creeping out, blinking at the sunlight and sneezing at the icy rain that had begun to fall yet again. Joyfully I crated the second hob and walked to the farmstead where the nephew had changed into dry clothes and was watching a children's programme on television. I was not unduly perturbed by the course of events for, in every group of ferreters, there is always the buffoon who has to stay to dig while the rest of the group move on to pastures new – and that buffoon is invariably me. What did cause dismay was when I next phoned the land owner to ask permission to ferret the land, I was told that the nephew had asked for, and been granted, exclusive ferreting rights on the farm. C'est la guerre – I could repeat a hundred similar stories. However since that time I have never engaged in that monumental piece of tomfoolery – night ferreting.

At this point in the book it seems expedient to forsake the subject of purse and long nets and seek another subject to discuss, and as the reader must now be aware that ferreting does not simply consist of ferret in/ rabbit out forays perhaps it is expedient to discuss that all too frequent of events, the lie up and how to deal with such a mishap.

9

The Lie Up

The ferret that goes to ground, facing the damp and foetid conditions of the burrow to deliberately find and drive out a rabbit so that the ferreter can net the coney, has yet to be born. A ferret is simply a partially domesticated polecat and when it finds a rabbit in the bowels of a burrow it seeks to kill it and to eat slivers of its flesh. Hence a ferret that hunts to satisfy the whims of its keeper would be a biologically aberrant beast that, should it become lost during a day's ferreting, would starve to death simply because it would neglect to kill and eat its prey.

Lie ups are inevitable – and hunters who claim that their ferrets simply race through burrows to push out the inmates are deluding themselves. Sooner or later almost every ferret will kill its prey and spend some time either examing its kill in the curious way all mustelids are wont to do, or to eat the carcass in the manner the Almighty has equipped them to do and such a delay, such a time spent underground with the quarry, is known as a 'lie up'. Thus, while lie ups are irritating, time consuming and damaging to the day's work they are nevertheless inevitable, and the purpose of this chapter is to suggest ways of how the delay might be reduced and how the rabbit and ferret might be recovered.

Ideally, a ferret would creep to ground, find a rabbit sleeping in its nest, awaken the said coney and harass the creature so that it is forced to quit the sanctuary of the burrow and bolt. The ferret's task then being complete the ferret follows the rabbit out of the burrow and is boxed. More often than not this is how the typical ferreting session progresses and the ferreter may survive many forays without the slightest hitch or indication of a lie up. It is usually then, when the tyro ferreter has come to believe that nothing can possibly go wrong and the tales of woe related by experienced ferreters can be disregarded, that a full blown lie up will occur – and every ferreter must be ready for such a crisis.

It is often said that ferreting is the sport of the silent, an activity for

Clearing a burrow before setting a net

those who do not require constant conversation to make their day endurable, and there is some truth in this belief. If the ferreting party arrives at the burrows they intend to ferret with the maximum clatter, talking noisily, allowing their dog to run amok at the burrow, then the rabbits below ground will be alerted to the dangers above ground and will be reluctant to bolt. It can, of course, be argued that the panic and terror a rabbit experiences when a ferret is put to ground exceeds the rabbits fear of bolting to a spot where dogs and humans are waiting – and to a certain extent this is true. However a rabbit that creeps to the mouth of a bolt hole, surveys the danger that awaits it, should it decide to bolt, will often retreat into the burrow to sit out the fury of a ferret rather than chance its luck by racing to the adjacent burrows. If a rabbit senses danger it is less likely to want to bolt than a rabbit that does not realise that danger awaits it on the surface. Hence a silent ferreting party is less likely to experience lie ups than a noisy group with badly behaved dogs and ferreters.

However ferreting sessions, in common with the best laid plans of mice and men 'oft gang a glae'. A ferret might be put to ground and will have little option other than to kill its rabbit. The rabbit might simply seek out a stop and sit, head inside the stop, haunches raised, to fill the passageway and wait until it is killed by the ferret, leaving the ferret to sniff, investigate and dine on the cadaver. However, while nothing can be done to prevent the ferret killing the rabbit, if the ferret is well fed and well watered (ferrets become inordinately thirsty when hunting) before it is put to ground, it will seldom stay to eat large quantities of its kill. It is a fearsome mistake to starve any ferret prior to hunting it for ferrets hunt rabbits simply because it is the nature of the wild polecat ancestors to do so. To starve a ferret to accentuate the hunting instinct is not only pointless but literally acts as an encouragement to the ferret to dine on the body of its victim to satiate its hunger. A well fed ferret will often kill its prey fairly quickly, sniff the cadaver, explore the various orifices of the coney and then fairly promptly leave the kill to pursue other quarry.

It is fair to state that the majority of lengthy lie ups occur late in the day, after the ferret has either bolted or killed many rabbits. It is often a surprise to ferreters to learn that ferrets too become fatigued and exhausted, but it is a fact that an adult polecat will kill and eat perhaps one rabbit every three or so days and be decidedly tired by its efforts dispatching this rabbit. Ferrets which bolt, kill or stay to six or more rabbits during the course of a typical day's ferreting are behaving in an unnatural manner so to speak and are fatigued, if not exhausted, by their efforts. When the ferreter, who is not aware of the physical state of his ward, continues to work the ferret at yet another rabbit, the ferret may well go to ground, kill the rabbit and promptly lie up on the corpse sleeping off its exhaustion without as much as tasting the flesh of its kill. Hunting a tired ferret is literally begging for the ferret to engage in a fairly lengthy lie up. I stop working a ferret if I notice that it displays a lacklustre attitude when entering a burrow and I dislike working a single ferret for a lengthy period of time. I have lost very few ferrets considering, that is, that I have owned ferrets for a great many years but I have seen many ferrets, owned by associates of mine, worked long after they were obviously very tired, lie up on the cadavers of rabbits and sleep off their weariness. I saw one of the best kittens I have ever seen lost in such a manner.

At that time I worked a bank of soil in Alrewas, and bolted many rabbits with my own ferrets. My associate who owned the rabbit hunting rights on this particular property had no ferrets at that time, and relied on me to furnish him any sort of sport, but, tiring of depending on my ferrets, he attended the small livestock market at Lichfield and bought a very under-nourished hob ferret – a white bibbed polecat ferret. Shortly after its purchase the hob scoured badly and became even more emaciated than ever but within weeks it had not only recovered but was starting to work with great enthusiasm, so that by the Christmas of that year the hob had become a most excellent and reliable worker. In the January of the following year he was so fearsomely overworked that he lost both weight and condition so that when the cold weather came he looked decidedly ragged and poor. In the early days of February we worked an entire Saturday using only the hob, as my associate was able to dictate which ferrets were to be used and he was too new to field sports to ever heed advice. The hob worked from early morning until night time and bolted not only many rabbits but two or three large rats. By night time the ferret looked decidedly tired and I realised that it was expedient to box up the hob and try another ferret. My associate was however of a different opinion and continued to put the exhausted hob to ground. Of course the hob killed and lay up on the corpse and as the warrens were very deep we declined to dig to the ferret. When a bad lie up occurs I can usually be fairly certain we will get rain for such is my luck. I looked around for stones to block the burrow so that I might return to the place the following morning and dig out the hob, but the burrow was a large one and it was not practicable to block the exits and entrances. I sat up all night waiting for the hob, and as I expected my associate complained that he did not like to leave his wife alone and left the field at around 7.00 p.m. It is in fact worth writing a book on the excuses some people will offer to excuse themselves from not sitting out the night when a ferret stays to ground – and I have heard most of these excuses.

My associate returned the next morning with one of my line ferrets – one of the few line ferrets I have ever owned that was totally reliable. I ran the line through every burrow but the bibbed polecat hob failed to appear and after listening to my associate deride me on how careless I had been not watching carefully enough to find his hob, and berating my hob for failing to move the white bibbed ferret, we returned home; my friend visibly pouting.

Several weeks later an old girlfriend of mine 'phoned to say that her daughter had found a mink and was keeping it as a pet. I was decidedly curious about the tale of a captive mink for, while I have seen some mink that could be handled, a wild mink is certainly not a suitable pet for a seven-year-old-girl. Hence I travelled to Alrewas to find the child was in possession of a white-bibbed hob ferret that obviously adored the girl. Of course I recognised the hob, but to separate child and ferret seemed sacrilege, besides which my failure to recover the hob had distanced me from his former owner. Some twelve years later I left Lichfield and paid all my old associates a visit. The child, now a university student and a startlingly beautiful woman, still sent home a pound a week to keep her very old and grizzled white-bibbed hob ferret.

Yet vigorous ferrets too will lie up and some fail to be able to return to the ferreter when they become trapped behind the cadaver of a rabbit. To those not initiated into the mysteries of ferreting it must seem bewildering that a ferret may easily find its way into a warren but yet be unable to find its way out. Equally as amazing as the fact that a ferret might be able to crawl over the back and head of a rabbit but be unable to crawl back. Yet once a ferret is placed in a burrow a series of curious, and often bizarre, happenings will sometimes take place. A rabbit might enter a stop, fill the hole leading to the stop with its haunches and invite a ferret to do its worst. While the ferret is clawing the rump of the rabbit in an effort to get over its back to administer a killing bite yet another rabbit, disturbed perhaps by the sound of thumping within the burrow, might also seek the sanctuary of the self same stop. Thus the ferreter might experience the phenomenon of a ferret attacking a rabbit only to be assailed by another rabbit pushing in behind it blocking its exit, and very occasionally its air. Add to this the fact that this tumult, with its accompanying squeaking and thumping, is taking place in the inky blackness of a burrow, the intensity of the darkness of which can only be appreciated by a miner who has experienced a power failure in the pit. Not surprisingly a ferret becomes trapped when such a series of incidents take place and even if the ferret wished to be clear of the cadavers that block its exit, it is unable to until, that is, it can literally eat its way free. Many times, particularly in the early part of the season, I have encountered two or three rabbits blocking the exit of the ferret thereby causing a lie up and when this type of situation arises the ferreter must either sit tight until the ferret emerges or dig to the ferret in order to recover it.

It may also surprise the tyro ferreter to realise that sometimes a ferret might become trapped behind a single rabbit and be unable to come to the surface. A rabbit, haunches filling the burrow, might now decide to sit out the storm but somehow or other the ferret, particularly if the ferret is a tiny experienced jill, might succeed in getting over the rabbit's back and administering a killing head bite. The ferret now finds itself at the stop end, its exit blocked by the cadaver of the rabbit it has just killed. During the struggle that preceded the death of the rabbit the coney may well have struggled violently and earth and stones might have fallen on top of the rabbit. The ferret now finds its exit blocked not only by the corpse of the rabbit but finds earth and pebbles completely sealing in the passageway and once again sealing off the air supply. Ferrets, unlike terriers seldom suffocate below ground for they have the inbuilt ability to survive damp airless conditions they have inherited from the wild polecat ancestors.

To reduce the time spent waiting for the ferret to emerge from such situations the ferreter must resort to digging for the ferret using sundry devices to locate the animal and its kill. There are no magic methods, no curious nostrums to prevent such incidents happening and should the tyro ferreter meet that ardent purveyor of country superstitions – the old poacher – he would do well to ignore the supposed wisdom proffered by these people regarding methods of getting a ferret to break a lie up.

Short term lie ups can however sometimes be broken by a number of somewhat macabre methods. A ferret that kills its rabbit in a passageway as opposed to a stop (a passageway has both exit and entrance) can sometimes be lured to the surface if the ferreter paunches a rabbit and leaves the pungent scent of the disembowelled rabbit to waft through the burrow. I have never favoured this method. It looks decidedly amateurish, smells badly and lends the foray an unpleasant aura for the rest of the day. Yet I freely admit I have seen this method used, and used successfully I must add.

Squeaking out is a technique that is often employed by ferreters – often without the ferreter realising why he is employing the technique. Squeaking consists of making a sound supposedly similar to the sound of a distressed or wounded rabbit and the ferret comes to investigate the cause of the commotion. This is often quite a successful method of causing the ferret to leave its kill, though whether the ferret believes the sound to be that of a rabbit is a moot point. My dislike for this method is engendered simply because I use dogs to mark burrows and the squeaking technique often disturbs the dogs or makes them less steady. When I am working my dogs in conjunction with ferrets I try my utmost to disuade any of my ferreting companions from squeaking out ferrets that have killed, or are in the process of killing, rabbits.

Drumming has a less disturbing effect on ferreting dogs, a far less unsettling effect than squeaking out. Drumming, like squeaking out, relies on the ferret's innate curiosity to make it work for I do not believe for one moment that the ferret believes that the sound of drumming or squeaking has been emitted by the rabbit. Drumming consists of the ferreter reaching into the burrow and drumming his or her fingers on the floor of the burrow. Supposedly this sound is said to mimic the sound of a rabbit kicking or running around the burrow. My own opinion is the ferrets simply leave their kills to investigate the source of an interesting and unusual sound. I have known ferrets leave their kills to seek out the source of the sound emitted by a ferret locator box. In the same way the sound of a spade blade struck atop of the burrow will sometimes cause a ferret to leave its kill – though sometimes the selfsame technique has the effect of unnerving the ferret and detering it from coming to the surface.

I have always believed this technique was one that was borrowed from badger diggers – and, prior to 1973, badger digging was not the heinous crime it might appear today. When the sound of a conflict below the soil indicated that the badger had seized or bottled up the terrier it was customary to bang the soil above the sound of conflict with a spade to deter the badger – and this sometimes worked, one should add.

A tried and tested method of causing the ferret to break its lie up (if that is it is able to do so and is not completely trapped in the burrow) is the use of a hostile and powerful hob ferret sometimes fitted with a line if the ferreter wishes to recover not only his erring ferret but also the carcass of the rabbit the ferret has killed. It is good policy for the ferreter who wishes to practice his art regularly to keep a large and powerful hob separate from the main ruck of ferrets. Such hobs kept separate and celibate often develop a surly attitude towards other hobs or jills. Such a hob entered into the burrow when another ferret has made a kill in the underground passageways will track and sometimes attempt to serve any jill or hob that is feeding on the kill. It is however essential to keep the hob separate from other ferrets so that it develops an antipathy to its fellow creatures. Often such a hob will not only drive off other ferrets, but follow them out of the burrow (often chattering loudly) and thus both ferrets can be boxed or crated.

Sometimes such a hob, particularly if the hob is a large and powerful animal, will 'free' a ferret that is trapped behind the cadaver of a rabbit. The hob is often curious about the rabbit it finds wedged in the mouth of a stop and may attempt to drag the cadaver to a spot where the hob can feed in peace. The ferret trapped behind the cadaver is thus often freed by the actions of the hob. Sometimes it is the presence of the ferret trapped behind the cadaver rather than the rabbit carcass itself that attracts the interest of the hob. At the time of writing I own a rather unreliable hob ferret that is kept separate from my colony of jills. He is grossly oversexed and endeavours to mate both males and females of his own species. In fact he shows little interest in the cadaver of a rabbit but will pull and tear at such a carcass if he suspects another ferret is lurking behind the corpse. The hob is seldom a reliable worker for one day he is all a warrener could desire and bolts each and every rabbit he encounters: the next day he may choose not to work and he will deliberately pass by rabbits in the burrow he is required to check. However whatever mood the hob is in he will actively seek out other ferrets lying up in the myriad passageways of a warren.

It seems a logical progression to move from the subject of a large hob used to shift less aggressive ferrets from kills to line ferrets, though the qualities of a good line ferret are many and varied. Prior to the perfecting of ferret locators, line ferrets were not only in great demand, but often fetched up to ten times the price of a small entered jill. Lest the reader should imagine that this is an excessive price to pay for a strong and powerful hob let me say that I have owned only one top grade line ferret in my life and I would not have sold him for any price. He escaped from his cage, was run down by a car outside my house and I felt his loss for many years afterwards. Such was the value placed on line ferrets before locators were perfected.

A line ferret is fitted with either a collar or a harness and from one of these devices is fastened a length of light but strong twine. This twine is knotted or marked every foot or so and should measure twelve or more yards in length. The hob, carrying his line, is entered into a burrow where another ferret has killed and refuses to come out and because the line ferret is usually worked on an empty stomach (and will stay to dine on the head of the cadaver) it is possible to dig to the hob and recover the kill.

I am enough of an anachronism to still find the use of a line ferret appealing, but line ferrets, or rather ferrets suitable for use as line ferrets, are seldom encountered these days. A line ferret must possess a unique amalgam of qualities to be first rate at his work. He must be large enough and strong enough to pull a line through a burrow that may be interlaced with the roots of shrubs and trees. He must be hostile to other ferrets of both sexes and more than willing to carry the battle to either sex. Yet he must be docile and easily handled by the ferreter. Such a ferret also needs to be shockproof for he must endure the clattering of digging yet resolutely stay with the kill until the ferreter delves to him. He must also be docile enough to allow himself to be lifted off his rabbit despite the fact that he is still hungry. Should one of the elements of the amalgam be missing then the hob becomes less effective and cannot be classed as top rate. If two or more of these qualities are noticeable by their absence then the animal becomes almost worthless. Perhaps less than one in a hundred large aggressive hobs becomes a first rate line ferret and the lot of a first rate line ferret is often far from enviable.

A line ferret must live separate from other ferrets so that when it encounters strange ferrets below ground it displays animosity to them. It must be hunted on an empty stomach – this is in fact the only time a ferret should be kept hungry before a hunt. More unpleasant still is the high death rate of ferrets that are kept specifically to carry a line. Lines snag on roots, are trapped between stones and ferrets are sometimes hanged when they topple over natural pit falls and are suspended by their lines. It can be argued that, while the ferret remains attached to its encumbering line, it can be recovered but this is not always the case. I have twice seen line ferrets thread their way through huge boulders becoming trapped behind rocks that were too heavy for a man to lift, and too large for the ferreter to dig around. Roots are however the line ferrets greatest enemy for many line ferrets come to grief attempting to negotiate roots. Roots snag lines preventing the ferret progressing further and present a problem when any ferret is worked on a line. At one time I worked a pine wood near Whittington, Staffordshire, a wood that adjoined a pasture that was closely cropped by the rabbits that had made their burrows beneath the pine trees. It was a nightmare of a place to work for the roots of the pines had caused the bedrock to crack and the rabbits had followed the lines of weakness and burrowed deep into the sandstone. Despite the quantity of rabbits the burrows held it was very dangerous to work the burrows for, once a ferret laid up, it required an excavator to retrieve the animal. I used my line hob twice in the burrows but both times he became tangled in the roots and it required a gargantuan effort to release him. Working the spot taught me a great deal. I became aware that no matter how competent a ferreter I believed myself to be there were spots that were unwise to ferret and as I dug frantically to my line hob that had been tangled below the pine roots I realised the value of a first rate line ferret.

Line ferrets are seldom worked these days for the importance of bushcraft, knowledge of the quarry and of the ferret has been superceded by use of the ferret locator and, lest the reader should imagine that I am decrying this remarkable piece of equipment, may I assure him I am not. Locators have assisted in the recovery of thousands of ferrets that would otherwise be living a wretched feral existence and prevented ecological disasters of the kind experienced when large numbers of mink escaped to the wild. On the debit side the skill and ethos of ferreting has suffered greatly because of the invention of the locator and perhaps, just perhaps, the nature of the typical ferreter has changed. In pre-locator times (a somewhat curious way of measuring time perhaps) the ferreter needed to be the most patient of men enduring hail, sleet and snow as he stead-fastly awaited the return of his ferrets. Such a ferreter needed the technical expertise enjoyed only by trout fishers and falconers a great knowledge of the sport blended perhaps with a saintly patience. Warreners often lived to great ages possibly because the nature of their employment slowed down their pace of living.

However the advent of the locator produced a new type of ferreter, and it has been argued possibly a new type of ferret. These days a ferreter can, without knowledge of the sport of ferreting, insert a collared ferret in a burrow, follow the progress of the ferret with a locator box and, as the ferret swiftly dispatches its quarry, dig to the source of the electronic signals. An hour's patient ferreting can be condensed into a brief, but frantic, ten minute search and recovery exercise – efficient and deadly, but scarcely a pursuit that has retained the aura of traditional hunting.

Worse still is the incidence of a condition I call locator dependency, a state of mind that, should a ferret be put to ground without its locator collar, or should the said ferret cast its collar while engaging its quarry, produces an anxious ferreter, a ferreter who is experiencing a state of anxiety similar to that of a woman who feels dread if the bus carrying her child is a few minutes late.

Might I forthwith admit to being the victim of a very bad case of locator dependency. Until the winter of 1987 I disdained the use of a locator and prided myself on my bushcraft, ferreting skills and, above all, my patience. When others have tired of waiting for a ferret and gone on to newer if not greener pastures I have waited. When fellow ferreters have quit monumental digs and gone home to warm beds and warm wives, I have dug on despite the wind and weather conditions that have tempted me to be elsewhere. However in the winter of the aforementioned year I attempted to dig a ferret from what first appeared a small easily dug burrow, but turned out to be a labyrinth of tunnels beneath tunnels. Torrential rain, icy rain the like of which falls only in the Highlands, fell throughout the day while I toiled to excavate tons of sandy soil. The sense of desperation that assailed me during that eight hour dig convinced me that despite my Luddite philosophy I would be wise to invest in a locator.

That evening I phoned Johnsons of Sheffield and invested in a collar and box and, while I will never be able to claim to be an expert in the use of such a device, I no longer need to rely on the gestures of my lurchers to direct me to the approximate vicinity of a lie up. I have however become locator dependent, reliant on the machinations of Deben Electronics rather than bushcraft. I now start to dig to my ferret a lot sooner than I need to perhaps and I experience an acute anxiety when I see a ferret not fitted with a locator collar vanish into a burrow.

Basically there are two kinds of locator: a locator that can detect the presence of a signal some eight feet below the surface and a more highly powered box that can detect that presence at a greater depth – some fifteen feet or so below the surface. Locator devices that are used to locate trapped terriers are invariably fifteen foot locators, while ferret locators are often devices that will receive signals from less of a depth. Having said this it is illogical to assume that rabbits will not delve more than eight feet to construct burrows. Fox earths are in fact more often than not simply enlarged rabbit burrows and more than once have I observed a ferret carrying a locator collar follow passageways that are so

A ferret that has killed and lain up on its kill
can be found with a ferret locator

deep as to render the ferret out of range of a fifteen foot locator box. I experienced one such an occurrence in Whittington Hurst in 1981 not long after Deben Electronics had perfected their locator devices. At that time my Luddite philosophy had made me very wary of electronic gadgetry and I had little experience of the marvels of locators. On this particular occasion I had been invited to witness these marvels by Raymond Edgar Harding, an extremely efficient ferreter from Birmingham. Ray's equipment was always immaculate. His ferrets were in top grade condition and his digging tools still retained their stainless steel appearance despite the fact they had experienced years of use. Ray had the technique of never uttering a word or casting a critical glance, but still making me feel that my dogs and equipment were falling to pieces and my house was actually more austere than it was. Ray had what is called an unfortunate manner, but it was only many years later that I realised that Ray made virtually everyone feel inferior.

Prior to meeting Ray I had witnessed home made locators in action and the results were often questionable for radio programmes were often as commonplace as bleeper sounds when such devices were used. Ray's device was top grade and functioned well, but during the first time I saw such a contraption Ray chose his burrows unwisely and his ferret killed and lay up under a tarmac road. At the second burrow, a spot near some deciduous trees, the ferret lay up deeper than the fifteen foot locator box could register.

Thus with two ferrets lying up in extremely difficult places to dig once more we sat out a cold and unpleasant afternoon that faded into night, and it was some time after midnight when the ferrets made their appearance. This incident wrongly coloured my impression of the value of locators and merely confirmed my Luddite philosophy. Had I the sense to realise that Ray had deliberately chosen difficult spots to ferret in order to demonstrate the efficacy of the locator I would have realised just how useful the locator kit was. As it was, the lie up, the icy night and the company of a man in whose presence I felt inferior coloured my views of mechanical ferret locators and it was to be years later that I would realise my mistake.

Locators are basically quite simple devices and worth many times their cost of purchase. However both the batteries that are fitted to the collars and the batteries within the receiver box run down and become useless with time and use, and once such batteries become very run down they produce inaccurate readings regarding the depth at which the ferret is lying up. I am one of the least mechanically minded men to have ever graced this earth, and for me technology ceased after the invention of fire and the wheel, but I find that batteries left in their housing, either in collars or in locator boxes are apt to drain or deplete their power more rapidly than batteries that are taken out and stored in clean dry boxes. After every foray I take off the collars, unscrew the heads of the battery attachments, thereby breaking the electrical circuit, and leave the tiny metallic batteries to rattle free in their housings. This lends a great deal of life to the collar batteries which, were the battery attachments left tightly screwed, would be constantly emitting signals and draining the power of the batteries.

Some advice on digging to a ferret now seems appropriate though personally I find digging to either ferrets or terriers an odious task. Once the locator box has signalled the presence of a ferret (plus collar) directly beneath it, I place the box directly above the signal and assess the depth of the ferret beneath the surface. If the ferret is lying up on its rabbit a foot or less, the hole that has to be dug to extract the ferret needs only to be a foot to eighteen inches in diameter. If the ferret is lying up some four feet below the surface a hole some yard or so in diameter must be dug, for it is often inordinately difficult to reach down into a narrow hole and extract a rabbit to which a ferret is adhering like a leech. The majority of diggers start with a hole that is patently too narrow to be workable by the time the digger has delved to the ferret and its rabbit. A hole that has to be constantly widened as the digger delves deeper and deeper is a great nuisance – and, like a watched pot that never boils, such a hole takes an inordinate time to dig. Thus it is better to start with a wide hole than to constantly have to widen the hole as one digs to the ferret. I invariably attempt to take off the surface turf in one piece rather than to chop the sod into a large number of small pieces. A single turf is easily replaced once the ferret and rabbit are extracted and the hole refilled, and it is always good policy to back-fill holes one has dug. Not only does the field resume its former features when sensible back-filling is practised but rabbits are more enthusiastic about recolonising a well-manicured earth than they would be in a burrow that is left open to the elements. Thus the use of devices and techniques of how to prevent lie ups, or perhaps to reduce the incidence of lie ups and loss of ferret and rabbit would be a more accurate description of the chapter. Now perhaps it is expedient to describe the use and training of the ferreters' dogs and whether or not a dog is an essential adjunct to the ferreter's team.

10

The Ferreter's Dog

Some weeks prior to penning this chapter it was a privilege to host three lady hunters on a research programme before publishing a series of articles that bore the working title *The Artemis Touch*. One of the ladies, an enthusiastic young ferreter called Sarah Smith, remarked that, despite the fact she owned one of the most magnificent lurchers, she often netted up rabbit warrens only to find the burrows were uninhabited – and rabbits will, in sandy soil, dig twenty burrows for every one they intend to inhabit. Now, just before the trio arrived I had occupied my time by re-reading Walsh and Lowe's *The English Whippet* and paused as I inevitably do at the sub-heading on page 109 'Ferreting with Whippets' that begins 'If you intend ferreting seriously you will leave the dogs behind' – a statement that never fails to amaze me for, without my lurchers, I should find ferreting the tracts of land I work difficult if not impossible. The visit from the three young ladies, if it did nothing else, convinced me of the error of the statement made by Mr Walsh and Madame Lowe.

I have few qualities about which I can boast. I am lazy, often shiftless and not particularly conscientious, but if I might find hope at the bottom of my Pandora's box of woes, the very best marking dogs I have ever seen are those I have trained and as a further boost to my rather shaky morale the very best marking dogs I have ever trained are the ones I presently own. It can be argued that the strain of lurcher has been kept by warreners for many generations, and hence has been eugenically tailored to perform exclusively as ferreting dogs, but the fact is that, with the correct training virtually any dog, lurcher, longdog, sighthound or any other breed can become a competent ferreter's dog.

Lurchers are traditionally the ideal ferreter's dog and for those who believe only diminutive mites of seventeen or so inches are the ideal ferreting dogs I say you are woefully wrong. However, before proceeding further, at an apparently disjointed pace, it might be well to discuss what are the qualities of a top grade ferreter's dog and how one might train such a dog to fulfil its duties.

A ferreter's dog must first and foremost be able to detect the presence of a rabbit in a burrow. If a dog is unable (rather than incapable, for no dog is incapable of marking a burrow) to perform this task it is of little use as a ferreter's dog despite the fact that the animal may have other sterling qualities such as speed and catching ability. Marking ability is an ingredient that is paramount in the chemistry of a first rate ferreter's dog and once a dog has acquired this skill the ferreter's dog becomes more of a pleasure for the numerous uninhabited burrows that have previously been netted can then be overlooked when the dog states that rabbits are not at home in these particular holes.

An important quality in a ferreting dog, one that is often overlooked by amateur ferreters, is attention span, or the ability of the dog to concentrate on the job in hand and not to allow its mind to wander and react to the events happening a hundred yards or so from the burrow the dog should be covering. A ferreting dog must lend a hundred per cent of its concentration process to the activities taking place beneath its feet. Should its attention stray for an instant, should it be alerted to a piece of paper fluttering in the breeze a furlong from the burrow a rabbit will invariably flash out of that burrow, catch the dog unawares and reach a place of sanctuary before the dog is capable of reacting to the appearance of the rabbit. My best ferreting bitch, a bitch the like of which it has never been my good fortune to breed before, and I should consider myself lucky to breed again, stands almost mesmerised as a ferret works the burrow and reacts with lightening speed when the rabbit bolts. Most of her catches are within ten yards of the burrow and her success rate at catching bolters is phenomenal. Horses and bullocks intrigued by the statue of a dog standing frozen like a Medusa-smitten beast are ignored as they tower above her and she is not even disturbed by the movements of a hare near the hedgerow or a pheasant pecking at grain in the corner of the field. Her mind is on the job in hand and on nothing else and because of this she is supremely successful as a ferreter's dog.

There is in fact considerable evidence to suggest that a lurcher used for ferreting should be kept to ferreting and not used for any other form of hunting. A tale will illustrate this point. In 1989 I bred a coursing dog by mating a top flight saluki male to a coursing greyhound bitch. Canaan, the resulting longdog, was an unruly, moody puppy low in intelligence perhaps but earnest in her resolve to catch game. She was entered by running her at ferreted rabbits and subsequently learned to mark well and freeze as a ferret was worked to rabbit. She never developed the instant lightening reaction of my best lurcher bitch but

No dog should be hostile to ferrets, and no ferret hostile to dogs

Canaan became a competent, though not great, ferreting dog. In 1991 she was sent for coursing training to Alan Hargreaves in Norfolk who has access to good hare country and an excellent record for fielding a dog in A1 condition. As she became accustomed to the appearance of hares, and learned to course them, Canaan realised her true vocation in life and began gazing around the field while Alan was ferreting. As she became more and more proficient at hare coursing she became less enthusiastic and less efficient as a ferreter's dog.

It is a moot point as to whether or not a ferreter's dog should work fearlessly in cover. It has been argued that many rabbits dig bolt holes in deep cover and a ferreting dog needs to cover such holes. Conversely a dog that dives into deep cover in an attempt to catch its rabbit is seldom successful at its work. A rabbit is able to negotiate tiny runs amongst bramble stolons, runs which would be far too small to allow even the tiniest terrier to follow. A dog that dives into cover at the first sight of a rabbit usually finds itself tangled in bramble stolons watching the rabbit flash away to the sanctuary of another bramble patch. As I write, my elderly lurcher Fathom is living out her last moments in the deep straw of my kennels and it looks highly unlikely she will last until morning. In her youth she was a mistress of the art of persuading a bolter to leave

111

cover. Fathom's technique was highly effective: she would race around the clump of bramble or gorse making half hearted 'puts' at the rabbit sitting in the centre of the cover, but Fathom seldom ventured into the thicket to bolt the rabbit preferring to make feints until the rabbit could be persuaded to bolt. At this stage of the hunt Fathom would be poised outside the clump and quite frequently caught the rabbit as it bolted.

Of course a dog that is totally cover-shy seldom makes a satisfactory ferreter's dog and some dogs are exceedingly reluctant to face thorn or, worse still, nettles. Some years ago I introduced beagle blood into my terrier strain in order to improve nose – and in this respect the outcross was eminently successful. However one of the quarter-bred beagle puppies was one of the most nesh puppies I ever produced. While its litter mates crashed after me through nettles Vanity, for so I had named the puppy, stayed well behind howling piteously when she felt the bite of the formic acid loaded needles of the nettles. I sent her to hunt service in 1970 and she distinguished herself well against fox and badger (at that time badger digging was considered to be a perfectly legal and respectable pastime). Vanity returned from hunt service not only a seasoned performer but cured of her cover shyness. Poor Vanity; during her next spell of hunt service she died after a particularly savage encounter with quite a small vixen.

However, the reader would be astounded to realise just how many dogs, dogs owned by quite famous hunters one should add, are very unsteady with ferrets. At one time I hired myself out to shoots working ferrets to bolt rabbits which were either shot or, more commonly, caught with dogs. When I worked alongside strange dogs, particularly terriers and lurchers, I lived in fear for the safety of my ferrets. The majority of terriers, and quite a few lurchers, are badly trained for their owners have neither the aptitude nor interest to break their dogs to ferret. Yet when Lucas hunted his pack of Ilmer Sealyhams, each and every dog was broken to ferret and there were virtually no accidents in the hunting field when Lucas fielded his team of terriers.

Would that I had continued to hunt with Jocelyn Lucas, for some of the encounters I had with wayward, unbroken terriers during the years I hired out were hair raising. It is amazing to realise the low esteem with which the more cavalier of working terrier men regard ferrets, some even consider them as disposable commodities I fear, and many times I had to throw myself atop of a ferret to protect it from the onslaught of a terrier. Spaniels were seldom troublesome with ferrets I should add – and most lived in awe of the creatures, but I have encountered more than one labrador retriever that, because it was not broken to ferrets, became an absolute menace while working with ferret.

Yet is is possible to break virtually any dog, no matter how fierce the disposition of the animal – to work alongside ferrets. In 1974 I saw one of the first American Pit Bull terriers to be imported into the country – a fearsome animal that had probably wrought red ruin in America where it had clearly been pitted against other dogs. The dog was totally steady with ferrets and allowed them to scamper over its ugly, scarred face and to peer into the pinnas of its cropped chewed ears. A bite from the brute would have crushed the life out of any ferret but the dog was rock steady with ferrets and seemed to actively encourage them to take outrageous liberties with him. The self same week I hired out to a much respected lurcher buff to bolt rabbits before the lurcher. I found it desperately difficult to fight off the dog and prevent it from killing my ferrets. All dogs should be carefully broken to ferrets before allowing the dogs to work alongside them and statements such as 'I'm sure that the dog will be steady with ferrets' should immediately alert the ferreter to the dangers of working this particular dog with ferrets.

If possible, the ferret keeper should break the dog to ferret as soon as the whelp leaves the nest; long before the dog has gained enough confidence to face down a ferret that displays any hostility to the puppy. Terrier puppies should be broken to ferret as soon as possible, for terriers are often very willing to avenge an insult (real or imaginary). Personally, I am decidedly wary of introducing a puppy to a ferret kitten and much prefer to use a seasoned ferret to break a puppy. At one time I used a very aggressive hob ferret to 'steady' puppies. If a puppy took liberties with him he nipped the whelp sharply before going about his business, but as the ferret grew older he became more and more trucculent with puppies. I ceased using him after what could have been an extemely unpleasant incident. As I was introducing him to the puppy the phone rang and I raced to answer it only to hear the cries of the terrified puppy that was being attacked by the ferret which was crawling over the head of the puppy in the manner in which it would seek to kill a rabbit. I became extremely careful about using the hob to break puppies since this incident.

It is always good policy to break a puppy to ferret in a situation that is far removed from the hunting field, for the presence of a rabbit may well excite the puppy and make it more difficult to break to ferret. I invariably choose a shed or empty room to break a puppy to ferret and simply place the ferret on the floor and chastise the puppy should the puppy show hostility to the ferret. It takes very few such sessions to break the puppy to ferret and the training process is always well worth the time spent.

At one time such was my state of penury that I took on unknown ferret-killing dogs and broke them to ferret. It was often an extremely difficult task though only once did I encounter a dog that simply refused to be broken to ferret, and to my eternal shame the bitch was a terrier I once bred. Once a dog kills a ferret the vice becomes as addictive as an opiate and a highly infectious vice at that. Perfectly steady dogs that observe another dog killing a ferret are less than steady during future hunts. Most ferret killers do in fact need a careful retraining programme, an aversion therapy programme that is tailored to make attacks on ferrets less appealing. I allow a ferret worrier to watch a ferret protected by a cage, and should the dog show an unhealthy interest in the ferret I jerk the leash attached to the dog's neck and yank the dog almost off its feet, uttering the cry of 'No' or 'Ferret' as I yank the leash. When I am more certain that I have some control over the dog and I am fairly sure the dog's animosity to ferrets has diminished I repeat this process when the ferret is running free of the protection of its cage, but I am extremely careful about leaving a ferret worrying dog alone with a ferret. It takes several weeks to cure a confirmed ferret killer of his vice and mistakes made during the training programme can lengthen the time it takes to cure such a dog. It is absolute madness to attempt to break a confirmed ferret killer of his problems in the hunting field when the dog is excited and the ferret fired with enthusiasm for the hunt. The chances are that even a casual ferret attacker may well retaliate if the ferret nips, or even menaces, the dog during the process of the hunt and few ferrets survive a bite from a dog. One thing is certain however, a dog must be absolutely steady with ferrets before it is taken into the field to work alongside these animals.

Teaching most dogs to mark rabbits, or rather to mark inhabited rabbit burrows, is simplicity itself and most dogs will usually self-train to perfect this technique. There are few dogs that will not at some time chance on a rabbit, spring the rabbit and after engaging the rabbit in an unsuccessful course see the coney disappear down a burrow. Few dogs will not actively try to scratch at the mouth of the burrow to attempt to dig out the rabbit and thus the technique of marking an inhabited burrow is born.

Once a dog marks an apparently inhabited burrow it is the responsibility of the ferreter to honour that mark by ferreting the burrow restraining the dog from digging, holding the dog close to the mouth of the burrow and inserting a ferret into the mouth of the hole the dog has just marked. The ferret will then endeavour to kill, but possibly succeed in bolting the rabbit, and the dog should be allowed to chase the fleeing coney. Now the dog experiences a degree of pleasure from the pursuit, albeit the fruitless pursuit, of the coney and in time the dog will associate the selfsame pleasure with the marking of a rabbit warren. I never teach a dog to mark by netting up the very first holes the dog indicates are inhabited, for the dog will experience very little pleasure from watching a rabbit becoming entrapped in the meshes of a net and hence it may take some time before it realises that by marking an inhabited hole it will trigger off a series of events the end product of which (the chase) it will find exciting. Hence until the dog is marking not only accurately, but eagerly, I forgo the use of nets and simply allow the dog to chase the rabbit that bolts.

Of course no ferreting dog should be unsteady with nets, for a dog that leaps on a rabbit encased by a net will not only damage the rabbit but severely damage the nets. While it is not impossible to have two dogs that are totally and simultaneously steady with nets, it is no mean feat to train two dogs to achieve this standard of obedience. While a dog may, and will, accept a human being as part of a hunting team, another dog is always regarded as a rival. When one of these dogs sees a rabbit entangle in the meshes of a net and 'breaks stay' to mouth the rabbit the other dog always become less net steady and a hurry on down process will often result from working two dogs together on a ferreting foray. The single-handed ferreting dog is always more efficient than the team of ferreting dogs that often have the reputation for being superlative rabbit catching dogs. In fact I have yet to see a team of lurchers that was anything other than chaotic and an embarrassment to their owner.

However, sometimes a dog that will do more than merely indicate the presence of a rabbit in a burrow and not seize a rabbit that is encased in nets is required – a dog that will pursue unnetted bolting rabbits or bolting rabbits that will throw the nets and attempt to escape to another burrow. For this task it would seem that the frail, yet deceptively tough, whippet would be the ideal sort of dog, that is of course until one examines the sort of terrain in which rabbits choose to nest. Few rabbits nest in flat billiard table country (though golf courses often sport a heavy infestation of rabbits). Rabbits need dry places to burrow and nest, land that is seldom sodden with water, and hence conies nest in dry banks, stone piles or in hedgerows elevated above the rest of the fields. More often than not rabbits will nest in well-drained wasteland adjoining fertile fields and in such wasteland, pit falls and death traps that can cripple or kill a running dog abound.

If such country has to be ferreted, a rather frail, finely built ferreting lurcher does rather less well than a less fleet but stronger, more heavily built, dog that is able to withstand the bumps and knocks a ferreting dog is virtually bound to sustain. My own lurchers are heavily built and not particularly fleet of foot (though during a twenty-five yard dash they are both quick and efficient) yet despite the fact I am forced to ferret some

Various types of lurcher can be used as ferreter's dogs

Even saluki hybrids can sometimes be used as ferreting dogs

of the toughest, most testing terrain in Britain my dogs are seldom injured and virtually never *hors de combat*. Yet I have noticed that more finely built dogs, lurchers infinitely faster than my own lurchers, are often terribly damaged when they are required to run this sort of terrain.

Longdogs are quite simply not geared to working with ferrets either by dint of their physique or because of their mental makeup. At the time of writing I own a splendid looking saluki-greyhound called Canaan which has won considerable honours in the coursing field. Canaan is a fast, very athletic, dog that puts up an excellent show against a hare, but is simply not geared to the sport of working alongside ferrets. Canaan has been taught to mark and is a fairly accurate guide to the nature and inhabitants of a burrow. However, here Canaan's usefulness ends. Her ability to be able to detect when a rabbit is due to bolt is very second rate and she is not as able to galvanise into flight as quickly as are my lurchers. True she has caught quite a few ferreted rabbits, but more often than not a chase ends with the sight of a slightly bewildered Canaan gazing down the mouth of a burrow into which a rabbit has just disappeared. Over a course of five or six hundred yards Canaan would be more than a match for a rabbit, but rabbits will seldom afford a dog such a lengthy course. Canaan is fast, but not quick, and there is a difference between fast and quick.

By contrast Phaedra is a lurcher bitch inbred to my now dead Fathom. Phaedra is quite heavily built, resistant to injury and able to catch at peculiar angles. She predicts the bolting of rabbits efficiently, is invariably in the right place when a rabbit chooses to bolt and over a distance of twenty-five yards she is devastatingly quick. In a course at hare Canaan would easily outrace her, but as a ferreting dog I have seen few to better her. Phaidra is quick rather than fast.

I am quite often required to work before television cameras and viewers often question the way I encourage dogs to 'fix' or freeze in front of a burrow to await the bolting of a rabbit, but such techniques are not only easily taught but highly efficient and effective. There are of course many ways of training a dog to stay in position while a rabbit is contemplating bolting. Many ferreters will insist on the dog adopting the down position while the ferret works below ground. However while it must be agreed that this method of fixing a dog is highly efficient at temporarily immobilising the dog it is scarcely an efficient position for the dog to adopt. Once a rabbit bolts, the dog has to make two distinct movements to be on its feet and able to pursue the rabbit and in the time the dog requires to be into flight, the rabbit is able to gain enough 'law' to be able to escape down a nearby burrow. Similarly a dog placed at a 'sit' position needs to make one distinct move to be on its feet and ready for pursuit. Conversely the dog placed at the freeze position at a certain point near or atop the burrow is able to be into full stride very quickly should the rabbit bolt.

I invariably teach the freeze technique to all puppies that I intend to work alongside ferrets. I usually put a ferret to ground in an inhabited burrow (a burrow down which I have seen a rabbit run to ground) and restrain the puppy by either holding the puppy's collar or restraining the whelp with a finger placed on the puppy's sternum. When the rabbit bolts I release the puppy and allow it to chase, and possibly catch, the coney and it requires only a short period of time to convince the puppy that it is more profitable remaining above or adjacent to the warren than wandering off in search of other interests.

Once the puppy becomes accustomed to staying in situ near the burrow I relax my discipline and allow the puppy to wander near the warren to chose the position to make its stand. Different dogs adopt different stances while a ferret is working its rabbit. Merab, the best lurcher I have ever owned, favours the half crouch of a pointer, a position from which she can dart forward and seize a bolting rabbit. Phaidra, Merab's granddaughter adopts simply a motionless standing position to await the bolter. Both positions can be efficiently employed though the half crouched pointing position looks a lot more effective.

Films of my ferreting sessions often invite considerable criticism for they usually depict my dogs stationed very close to, and in front of, the entrances to burrows – and this position is apparently contrary to the good training advice proferred by many ferreting/lurcher books. I am, I confess, a field sports heretic but I have found stationing my dogs in such positions highly efficient. My dogs so stationed are required to remain motionless and freeze in such positions lulling the rabbit into a false sense of security, for rabbits are seldom deterred from bolting by the presence of an alien shape in front of the burrow providing, that is, the alien shape is immobile. I have in fact many times observed a rabbit attempt to bolt between the feet of a 'frozen' lurcher and Merab has become extraordinarily adept at dealing with such bolters. In fact some twenty-five per cent of the rabbits my dogs catch are snapped up within ten feet of the mouth of a burrow. This method of catching is a technique most dogs can learn, but only if the dog is standing near to, or directly in front of, the burrow. I have observed sensible experienced terriers develop this snatch technique while ratting, often allowing the rat to creep completely out of the burrow before snatching up the fleeing rat. Once a dog is sensible obedient and has lost the excitability one associates with puppyhood it is wise to allow the dog to make use of its natural intelligence and bushcraft, and develop certain unique qualities that can assist in the capture of quarry. Dogs kept under a martinet training regime are not only unhappy but become decidedly inefficient at working with ferrets, relying on commands from the handler rather than the dogs natural ability. Training will sharpen and improve a dog's performance, but unless the dog is allowed to exploit the skills it has acquired the animal will seldom become more than a second rate ferreting dog.

It takes many years to train a competent ferreting dog that will actually work with, rather than alongside, ferrets but once a dog is trained it cannot be priced. It becomes an essential adjunct to any ferreting team, and the ferreter becomes lost without the animal. Lamping lurchers are two a penny and frequently sold, for it requires but little skill to train a dog to run down a beam of light and snatch up a rabbit. To train a competent and reliable ferreting dog takes so much of a ferreter's time that it is exceedingly rare to see a really well-trained ferreting dog offered for sale. A lamping lurcher is over the top as a worker by its seventh year – though some dogs are worked until they are much older. A ferreting dog, a well-trained lurcher with a good nose, will give much longer service. My old lurcher Fathom was worked alongside ferrets until she was seventeen years old and retained her incredible nose until her dotage. The time I took training her was certainly well spent.

However, it is very difficult to train a replacement ferreting lurcher alongside an experienced and competent dog. All manner of evils will result from such a practice. Retrieving, fetching a caught rabbit to hand certainly suffers if two or more dogs are fielded together. At the time of writing I work two lurchers, Merab and her granddaughter Phaidra. Both are natural and eager retrievers but when worked together matters go seriously awry. When a rabbit bolts both pursue the animal and should one or other of the lurchers catch the rabbit, the other lurcher too will invariably attempt to seize the catch. Both attempt to carry the rabbit to hand and it is virtually inevitable that the carcass will be bruised and damaged. Should one lurcher catch while the other is pursuing another bolter, the dog with the catch is reluctant to retrieve its rabbit to hand lest the other lurcher attempts to seize it. The day sours badly when I enedeavour to work both lurchers together and the essential activities take on a ragged look that makes me feel decidedly uncomfortable. I am not a number counter, one who delights in the number of rabbits caught during a day's hunting, for I value style and hunting panache in my lurchers. Hence the working of two or more lurchers together is neither efficient nor spectacular to watch.

Let me conclude this chapter by saying that I am particularly careful about allowing a lurcher to take liberties with a ferret that has just followed a bolter from a burrow. Such a ferret, particularly an inexperienced kitten, is often heated by the conflict it has just experienced and may nip a dog that pays the ferret attention. My own lurchers are trained to be decidedly wary with ferrets and will indicate that a ferret is about to leave the burrow by turning away from the ferret in an effort to avoid any form of conflict with the creature. A dog that is slightly wary, a shade apprehensive about ferrets, is often the best type of ferreting dog. Frankly, I rather worry about dogs that are allowed to take liberties with ferrets. I have seen so many ferreters actively encourage dogs to retrieve live ferrets to hand and while this relationship and trust twixt dog and ferret is commendable should this particularly sociable ferret become lost, and should the ferreter require to replace this ferret with another adult, the new ferret may well be terrified by being carried about by a dog and react accordingly. I have always encouraged my lurchers to have a healthy respect for ferrets.

11

Ratting

Most modern ferreting books seem disinclined to discuss the subject of ratting with ferrets, and some writers seem decidedly antipathetic about using ferrets to bolt or kill rats. However it is easy to understand why keepers who are concerned for the welfare of their ferrets are reluctant to allow their ferrets to tackle rats; for rats in addition to being carriers of some of the deadliest diseases known to man are fearsome biters that can and will inflict hideous wounds on a ferret that ventures into a rat burrow. During the twenty-three years I ran a rat pack (a pack of terriers I kept specifically to hunt rat) I saw rats inflict gaping wounds on the heads and legs of terriers, wounds seemingly out of proportion to the size of the rat inflicting these wounds. Most of the huge rips occurred when a rat had seized the face of a terrier attacking it and another terrier had plucked at the rat's body. However, I have also received bites from rats and can attest to the depth and width of these wounds. It is indeed small wonder why many conscientious ferret keepers are unwilling to encourage their ferrets to seek out and destroy rats. Thus in view of the opinion of several eminent ferreting authorities on the morality of hunting rats with ferret I begin a chapter 'Ratting' with some trepidation.

Despite the fact that, at the time of writing, there is a craze to breed tiny and sylph-like ferrets; hobs, even very tiny hobs, are seldom efficient at the task of bolting rats. Perhaps there are aspects of sexual dimorphism that have yet to be explored that can account for the reluctance of many hob ferrets to take the battle to a fully grown rat, but certainly I have observed tiny elf-like jill ferrets rush to and seize a fully grown rat that has caused a hob to back out of a crevice and find it has better tasks to attempt elsewhere. Hobs are certainly not as useful at working rats as jill ferrets. Tom Evans of Blaegarw once told a tale of the days when few courts were totally aware of the ramifications of the 1911 Protection of Animals Act – an Act that gave the rat some, albeit it scant, protection. Tom mentioned a village eccentric who kept several large hob ferrets in a barrel (many ferreters disdained the use of ferret cages when suitable barrels could be obtained) and two or three times a week tipped live adult rats into the mess of ferrets. The rats would usually run over the backs of the sleeping hobs and attempt to scale the walls of the barrel. Yet despite the fact that young grey rats were killed and dismembered by the hobs, an adult rat would often remain alive for several days in this hideous pit of death for the hobs seemed reluctant to attack these rats. When such a rat died of shock (and what an incredibly hideous death for any animal to endure) the hobs ate the cadaver voraciously. Yet these hobs were apparently fearful of, or at least reluctant to attack, live healthy adult rats.

Yet such rats thrown into a cage of adult healthy jill ferrets would receive short shrift from these females who would invariably attack their prey with great zest and dine on the kills. Indeed prior to the 1911 Protection of Animals Act there were several rat pit exhibitions involving a ferret killing rats against the clock so to speak, disposing of up to a dozen terrified huddled adult rats in a given period of time. A hob ferret was hardly ever used for such exhibitions, for jills seem to display a natural antipathy to rats, an antipathy that is sometimes noticeable by its absence in hob ferrets.

Some hobs will work rats, particularly in burrows which are fairly wide and easily negotiated by the hob, under floors of sheds, crevices in cavity walls etc., or in burrows excavated by other creatures – rabbit warrens near rubbish tips or farmsteads. However to attempt to use hobs, even small jill-sized hobs for serious and regular ratting is to court disaster and to invite failure. Hobs are just not psychologically geared for such outings and usually put up indifferent shows against strong healthy rats.

It has been argued that the diet of the wild European polecat male may be slightly different from that of the female and this aspect of sexual dimorphism may well be the reason why female ferrets take more readily to ratting. However this argument too has its shortcomings. Wild polecats, both males and females are shy of tackling hostile adult rats that are willing to take the fight to an attacker. Lorenz argues that any predator that attacks prey that will put up a fight is likely to sustain injuries that over the course of a few brief months will render the predator unable to hunt. Thus no meat eater is likely to seek out quarry that will retaliate fiercely and a healthy strong adult female (and this will be explained presently) rat will fight with desperate fury.

Thus it is patently obvious that, unlike the rabbit, the rat can scarcely be considered suitable quarry for even a jill ferret. The ferreter must be *au fait* with this fact from the start for in no time the jill too will be aware of the fact that the rat is not a suitable foe with which to battle and from that moment on the jill will refuse to enter rat lairs even to hunt out young grey rats that will seldom offer her a serious fight. Henceforth the jill must be relegated to the task of rabbiting and ferrets will continue to work rabbits until their dotage despite the rough and tumble the jill will encounter in a rabbit burrow.

The jill will usually meet her Nemesis in the form of an adult female rat, for bucks, even dominant bucks that rule a colony with an awesome dominance, will rarely fight it out with a ferret. Some bucks will usually bolt as soon as the ferret is placed in the mouth of a burrow and even when such a buck is backed into a blind stop he will usually choose to sit out the storm by pushing his head into the earth of the stop and, like a cornered rabbit, invite the ferret to do her very worst. She usually will, and often buck rats are killed with the very minimum effort by quite young ferrets.

Not so the female rat I am afraid. A doe rat may well be pregnant even before she reaches adulthood and days before she kindles she will prepare a nest by gathering paper, sticks, grass and straw and making a warm secure den in which to rear her young. She will then defend this nest against all comers, be they other rats, stoats, weasels, ferrets, cats or dogs. I cannot resist relating a tale that illustrates not only the fighting fury such a female may display, but my own sheer stupidity. During my late thirties I became exceedingly adept at catching live rats with my hands – a symptom of sheer lunacy that may well have been induced by the fact there was precious little else I could do, apart from catching rats by hand. However one May a Dutch television company, that obviously had an interest in good old British eccentrics, requested permission to film a rat hunt and required a hand catching sequence to lend spice to what turned out to be an extremely unpleasant programme. To cut a long story short I failed to live-catch until late in the evening when a rat raced up a board and into a hole in the roof and remained there, its tail hanging outside the hole. I attempted to grab the tail but as I did so a nesting doe watching from within the hole dashed out, bit my thumb and endeavoured to pull my hand into the lair. Her bite was hard and furious and my thumb nail was split assunder by the pressure of her jaws. Camera and sound teams promptly arrived to film my discomfort and the end result of the project was a sleazy film that did the rounds of low-grade television stations throughout Europe. Such is the fury of a nesting doe and such a demon a small slender jill ferret may be required to face in a dark and narrow lair. Small wonder ferrets will often decide to quit ratting after a bad mangling from such a Gorgon.

A nesting doe remains unapproachable and furiously hostile to in-truders until her young are two weeks old and are no longer naked and helpless, after which she will bolt as though terrifed accompanied by her grey youngsters when a ferret enters the lair. Curiously, ferocious does that will guard a nest against all comers will offer a ferret little fight once her young are weaned and capable of fleeing before a ferret. Does will seldom stay to defend furred young that are beset by ferrets. Yet ratting with ferrets during the summer months is thwart with danger for the ferrets, for rat does are wont to draw nests every three or four weeks during the warm months of the year. Hence a ferret is in constant danger of meeting one of these harridans if it is worked to rat from March to November. I should add I have never yet had a jill ferret badly bitten during a winter time ratting session and have observed how easily rats will bolt before a ferret from the first frosts until spring.

When I hunted rats some four days a week with my terrier pack and ferrets – and, I hasten to add, sunk any career prospects in teaching without trace because of my interests, I made a point of never entering a ferret to rat until the jill had experienced a full season of rabbiting, or until the New Year when the jill was usually well grown and mature enough to withstand the attack or retaliation of an adult rat. Yet, despite the precautions I took, and no matter how careful I was about entering ferrets to rat there was seldom a season when I had enough willing ferrets (ferrets that had not been deterred from attacking rats by the fury of some nursing doe) to work until August. So from August until the New Year my ratting forays were carried out at night and I eschewed the use of ferrets during these hunts.

Yet some jills will work rat with great regularity without quitting cold so to speak. Three such jills spring to mind. In 1965 I bought a small rather evil-tempered jill from a pig keeper in Swinton, Yorkshire, after the jill had reared a litter of twelve kits that had fed on the cadaver of a pig that had died from some disease that had turned the face of the pig an evil blue/black colour. The jill was prickly, unpredictable and sometimes spiteful with people but was a wonderful worker that survived for several seasons until a dog, whose owner had assured me the terrier was steady with ferrets, killed the jill with a single bite. The second jill attracted my attention as I passed a ferret cage in Doncaster market and I have never regretted the caprice that induced me to buy her. She served me well for several seasons and her progeny were still at my ferretry in Lichfield some twenty years later. My third jill, also a polecat, a dark fitch, I bred from the progeny of the above mentioned jills, and she ratted and rabbited for some six seasons until a useless Border terrier nipped her when she escaped from her pen and found her way into the terrier's kennel.

Yet for every jill that would withstand a bad drubbing from a rat and still be ready for a rat hunt I have known ten that would never again face a rat once they were badly bitten by what invariably proved to be a nesting or suckling doe rat. Hence if the ferreter intends to hunt rat with regularity he will need quite a few jill ferrets kept for preference in two cages; one cage for ferrets that have quit working and the other for those still eager to hunt rat. I say two cages for such was my enthusiasm for ratting that it was my practice to reach into my ferret cage before first light and pick up any ferret that came to hand. I hasten to add that my active work force was seldom enough to continue ratting by August but the quitter pen 'ranneth over' so to speak.

At this juncture perhaps it is time to mention that most peculiar of creatures, the greyhound ferret, as baffling a chimaera as the Smithfield collie – and possibly equally as extinct. At one time a distinct type of ferret was used to work rat, a long lean but muscular and heavy ferret that was not only constitutionally equipped to work rat (yet only the jill ferrets worked rat I should add) but usually a more determined type of ferret that would often attempt to face down a bedding-drawing doe rat. The faces of such ferrets were often sharp and pointed and should the reader suspect that such features meant a weak and snappy jaw I should add that greyhound ferrets had a reputation for being hard and furious biters. Most greyhound ferrets were white, but dark polecat and sandy ferrets were not unknown. In fact the first greyhound ferret I ever saw was an ugly ginger sandy ferret that was used to bolt rats from the dry stone walls of pigsties that sprouted around the hills adjacent to my South Wales valley home. The jill had been bought from Leslie Dyer of Ely, Cambridgeshire, a livestock breeder who contined to advertise greyhound ferrets until the 1960s after which I found no bona fide breeders continuing to advertise these long, lean, aggressive ferrets.

I can only assume what happened to these ferrets and I can offer no proof for my assumption. During the 1950s myxomatosis literally wiped out the rabbit population of many counties where warrening or professional rabbit catching was once a profitable business, and it became virtually impossible to sell ferret kittens bred from good rabbit catching parents. For a number of years the majority of ferret kittens were sold as greyhound ferrets and after a while it became customary to refer to any white ferrets as 'greyhounds' despite the shape, size and disposition of these ferrets. As I have mentioned I believe that in the 1960s Leslie Dyer, a stock breeder from Ely, Cambridgeshire, abandoned advertising genuine greyhound ferrets simply because the majority of white ferrets were being passed off as 'greyhounds'.

During the 1950s John Collingwood's name was almost synonymous with ratting ferrets and I saw a great many excellent and typey ferrets from his emporium. Collingwood 'bought in' litters from jills he sold, mated to one of his own hobs – buying cheap, but selling dear perhaps but always offering to buy back litters of his breeding for he had an apparently bottomless market for his stock. For about six years I bred Collingwood-type ferrets – polecats streaked with grey and white hairs; unattractive by today's standards perhaps but renowned workers to rat.

I bred to supply Collingwood, quite often supplying him ten litters of kittens a season for which he paid me a pound a kitten and sold them for five pounds a ferret and I had no complaints about my dealings with this quaint old man. I found it difficult to sell ferrets whereas Collingwood found it remarkably easy, so all in all it was an amicable arrangement and I was never cheated or short-changed when I took the litters to his home. In 1973 the hob I used to sire these litters died and I replaced him with an almost identical hob Moses Smith had purchased at Lichfield livestock market. In the August of that year I took my litters to sell to Collingwood, but after a mere half glance at them he refused to buy, for he realised they were not from his pure line. He never did business with me again for I feel he felt I had cheated him by passing off inferior ferrets. It was a pity for I both knew and liked old man Collingwood. In 1987 I was given a ferret by a Durham breeder for a friend of mine, Jerry Boyle of Beauly. The hob was reputedly Collingwood-bred but while it had the same rather dirty polecat colouring the long sinuous shape and mean face of the strain I had once known was noticeable by its absence. I suspect that greyhound ferrets became extinct shortly after Collingwood died. I never see the type he favoured these days.

When ratting with ferrets was more socially acceptable than it is today, it was customary to feed these ferrets almost exclusively on a diet of rat meat, allowing ferrets to feed on the whole cadavers of adult and young rats. Ferrets thrive on such a diet, though rats are carriers of sarcoptic mange. It was usual practice to cut off the scaly tails of the rats before presenting them to ferrets. Throughout my entire life I never once saw a ferret eat the tail of an adult rat though no doubt a hungry ferret would consider such fare. It was considered that a rat-fed ferret afforded a longer ratting life than a ferret fed on other viands. However it should be pointed out that once a ferret quits cold at ratting no amount of rat meat will rekindle its desire to hunt rats again. However, ferrets will maintain weight and grow well when fed on a diet of whole rats and I reared many litters of ferrets exclusively on rat flesh.

I avoid feeding the cadavers of rats that have died of causes unknown however, and feed only the healthy rats my terriers have killed. Rat corpses may well have died after ingesting rat poison and ferrets too succumb to such poisons when they eat the meat of poisoned rats. Most rat poisons such as Warfarin or allied poisons cause rats to die from some form of internal bleeding and these poisons are quite deadly to ferrets. At one time I fed some sixty pounds of whole rats a week to my ferrets and never once did such food cause a single ferret to ail in any way.

The purpose of entering a jill into a rat warren is to cause the rats living in the warren to bolt rather than to allow the ferret to kill the rats below ground – though on occasions this will almost certainly happen. Hence I usually enter one ferret at a time into a warren as this method of ratting seldom bottles up a rat preventing its escape and causing it to fight to the death. I usually approach the rat warren as silently as I can, keeping my dogs stationed at strategic positions while I send the jill to ground. A rabbit alerted to the dangers above ground will sit, head into the stop, and sit out the attack from a ferret. A rat alerted to the danger will also seek the sanctuary of a stop but will sometimes face the ferret head on and may possibly fight it out rather than meekly submitting to the onslaught of the ferret. Two ferrets inserted into the same warren may possibly prevent a rat from bolting and cause the most dreadful of battles. Hence it is wise to work only one ferret in a single warren no matter how large and labyrinthine that warren might be.

In such warrens, particularly if such lairs are situated in the interstices of the foundation of a building, ferrets can and do get lost. Yet it is a questionable practice to fit any ratting ferret with a ferret locator. Quite often rat warrens are only just wide enough to allow a small jill ferret to negotiate the passageways and a ferret fitted with a locator is encumbered by a locator collar which may prevent the ferret from getting to its rat. Yet it can be argued that when a rat warren is extensive or situated in a rubbish dump (where rat lairs may be extremely extensive) nowhere is the use of the locator more needed. Yet if the tunnels of the warren thread their ways between tree roots or through the crevices between large stones a locator collar is a particularly dangerous piece of equipment. Frankly, while I freely admit that I feel positively naked rabbit hunting without fitting a ferret with a locator collar I never fit such a collar around the throat of a ratting ferret.

A skirmish between a ferret and a strong healthy doe rat is particularly exhausting to the ferret and a ferret entered to a succession of rats is almost certain to quit cold and refuse to tackle another rat once it becomes exhausted. A wild polecat might engage in a monumental struggle against an adult rat perhaps once a week and, once it kills that rat, it feeds upon the cadaver and only seeks to hunt again when the kill is eaten. To expect a ferret, a domesticated polecat, often in a less fit condition than its wild ancestor, to wreak mayhem on a great many rats in a days ferreting is expecting quite a lot. Yet some ferrets are deadly rat killers. Fudge, one of my best ferrets, slew eight large strong rats on a day's hunting on a rubbish pile near Tamworth and emerged with a mere scratch or so for her troubles.

On the subject of ferrets leaving a rat warren after a hard and testing battle with rats, the ferreter should be careful about how he handles his wards until, that is, he is certain about the way his ferret is likely to act after a conflict. Some ferrets will readily accept being handled immediately after a furious battle with a rat. Others are less tolerant. Megaera, an evil looking one-eyed jill I bought at Swinton in the 1960s, was particularly adept at tackling rats and killed them swiftly and efficiently. Yet immediately after a battle she would emerge from a rat lair, tail in a gale, and defy me to reach down and pick her up. She would adopt the threatening posture for several minutes before reverting to her normal calm self again, but woe betide the hand that reached for her before she was ready to be picked up. Worse still, woe betide the dog that was stationed near the burrow when Margera emerged from the rat lair – however more on that subject presently.

A ferret that has been badly bitten by a rat is in considerable danger for the saliva of rats is riddled with numerous deadly bacteria. At one time I used a penicillin ointment to treat bites, only to find that the Hungerford ferret monograph (Lewington) states that ferrets are allergic to penicillin. However, wounds inflicted by rats need careful cleaning and disinfecting lest they fester and cause ferrets great distress. It is also worth noting how dangerous a bite from a ferret that has eaten rat flesh or bitten a rat to death can be to the ferreter. The sane and sensible ferreter should in fact try to prevent any contact with rats either directly or via a ferret that has worked the tunnels of a rat warren. Ferrets frequently acquire both fleas and mange mites when working rats. Both can infect the ferreter and cause unpleasant and dangerous infections.

If ratting ferrets should enter a warren and drive out rats, rather than kill them in the dark confines of the lairs how, the reader might ask, should the ferreter catch the rats that bolt before a ferret, and it should be borne in mind that a rat leaves its burrow (when coaxed to do so by a ferret) at an astounding velocity, and is well aware of where it is heading long before it leaves the lair. It is possible, well just possible, to shoot such rats as they flash between lairs but to do so successfully would require the skills of a trapshooter with the reactions of a Chinese martial art film stunt man. Frankly I have observed only damage to property and precious little else as a result of attempting to shoot ferreted rats. I have many times seen successfully conducted rat shoots, but only when hunters have stalked rats when these rodents were feeding abroad. Ferreted rats bolt far too quickly for most gunmen to shoot. A tale will certainly illustrate my point. In the 1970s I hosted a band of air gunners and we hunted a poultry farm two nights a week stalking feeding rats or shooting rats that became illuminated in a beam of light shone on the nighttime feeders. The team shot as many as thirty rats a night. They shot only twice at ferreted rats and scored so poorly that never again did I stage a ferret-aided rat shoot.

Nailing ferreted rats with sticks can be an extremely effective method of killing rats if, and this is a big if, the ratting team are calm, sensible and adhere to rules and regulations imposed on them by a team leader. My own ratting team stayed with me for many years and quite frequently we eschewed the use of dogs and simply struck at the rats with sticks. Some of the women members of our team became extremely adept at striking bolting rats, far more reliable than any of the males in the group in fact.

The sticks are implements used to stop or knock down rats and are of course all important. I made it a rule never to allow anyone to brandish anything akin to a club or a stick longer than two foot six inches. I found hazel twigs one and a half inches thick to be the ideal implements to club bolting rats for these twigs were light, strong, yet sufficiently heavy to deal a rat a blow and to stop the rodent in its tracks. Club-like weapons are too heavy to wield and invariably cause damage to property or, worse still, any dog that is unlucky enough to run beneath a descending blow from such an implement – and I shall deal with the problem of working amongst dogs presently. Likewise, a thin wand-like stick offers little stopping power and those who wield such weapons invariably look quite ludicrous and ridiculous wildly whipping at rats. It might be of interest to the reader that I cut and dried my hazel ratting stick in 1966 in Maltby, Yorkshire and finally burned the remains of the stick in 1985 when I disbanded my ratting pack. Such is the use a properly cut and dried ratting stick will give. I lost my stick for a month when the weapon fell in a slurry pit at a poultry farm in Sutton Coldfield and felt a curious elation when I recovered the implement a month later. I had become so used to the stick that I felt almost naked without it.

I have seen many rats entrapped in the meshes of ratting nets – specially constructed fine-meshed nets, specifically tailored to catch rats. Likewise I have caught many rats in rabbit nets when rats have bolted from rabbit burrows by dint of ferrets. However, I have had very little success entrapping rats in specially built rat nets. These rat nets, and I freely admit that I have met people who are very adept at catching rats in these meshes, are usually custom-made by net makers. My own rat nets, indeed all my nets, rabbit, purse and gate nets were hand made by the Jackson family and while I admit I gave my rat nets away (a rather churlish gesture as they were a Christmas present from the Jacksons) the hunter to whom I gave my nets put them to much better use than I ever did.

I seldom try to extract live rats from a rat net. The process is often messy and incredibly hazardous as enmeshed rats will bite with great fury and often damaging to the meshes of the net. I simply give the tangled rat a short sharp blow to kill the rodent before attempting to untangle the corpse. Furthermore it is exceedingly difficult to untangle a live rat from a net for the feet of this rodent, and also the long scaly tail, become hopelessly tangled in the meshes of the net. It does in fact often require considerable patience to untangle even a dead rat from a net and a lot more patience (and juggling skills) to extract live rats from the same nets.

However the most effective way of catching ferreted rats is to work dogs in conjunction with ferrets and this subject merits a separate chapter.

12

Ratting Dogs

During the many years I ran my rat pack I was defeated in rat hunting contests only twice: once by a poodle cross-bred and the other by a mongrel pointer. Both times I was severely thrashed and made to look mildly ridiculous. Yet I would never recommend that a person conside-ring taking up the sport of ferreting rats should use anything other than a terrier, though I have seen whippets kill rats with great skill and enthusiasm. The fact is that terriers are mentally and physically geared to hunt rat. They are usually of quicksilver disposition, utterly game (and rats bite fearfully hard) agile and small enough to dive into the crevices in which ferreted rats usually seek to hide when they bolt before a ferret. Quite tiny terriers often make exceedingly good ratters and many times I have fielded terriers of five or six pounds in weight which caught and killed rats with great enthusiasm, though I confess that these terriers looked very much the worse for wear at the end of an evening.

I have never really rated the much vaunted Staffordshire bull terrier as a ratting dog though many writers claim these dogs to be the only really conscientious ratting terriers. Bull terriers have terrific jaws that kill rats quickly and neatly. They are also game enough to endure awful havoc of the sort a rat, sitting it out in an almost inaccessible crevice is likely to inflict on the dog. What bull terriers usually lack is mobility and agility and while the powerhouse dive of a bull terrier is impressive to watch, it is seldom that such a leap is as efficient as the delicate 'snatch' of a more lightly-built terrier. At one time I worked my own breed of terrier alongside a pair of Staffordshire bull terriers bred down from the fabulous Black Monarch, a famous stud dog of the time. My own terriers caught, killed and hunted up far more rats than their heavier rivals though after a while the barging and jostling tended to unnerve the more effete of my terriers. After a while I stopped inviting the hunter who kept those solidly built pit dogs.

I have seen some excellent Cairn and West Highland White terriers worked to rat and in many ways this type of terrier is as good as any as a ratter. These terriers have strong jaws, great agility and the correct shape to crawl into tangles of rubbish to dispatch rats. At one time Joan Hancock, of Sutton Coldfield, kept some truly excellent ratting Cairn terriers that were hard to fault at ratting amongst farmyard equipment. The fact that this small team of Cairns seldom caught high scores of rats was due to the fact that Joan was often too busy to hunt them, rather than the reluctance of the Cairns to work.

Fell terriers, Jack Russells and at one time Border terriers were amongst the most popular ratting terriers employed by hunters. Fells, rightly or wrongly, have a reputation for having poor noses and nose is an absolutely essential requirement for a first-rate ratting terrier. Many ratters still swear by that mish-mash of breed types known collectively as Jack Russell terriers but in recent years constant infusions of Lakeland terrier blood have reputedly done little to improve the nose of these, otherwise excellent, ratting terriers.

My own particular preference is clearly for the type of terrier I keep and breed, a breed type now known as Plummer terriers. The type developed from stock I kept over the many years I bred terriers. Basically the type consists of a mixture of beagle, bull terrier, fell terrier and Jack Russell, the aforementioned ingredients added to give nose, courage, type and agility. The type began to breed true in the 1960s and is now breeding as true as many strains of registered terrier. Despite the fact that my team of terriers ratted four nights a week, the type was developed as an all-purpose hunting dog and few dogs working in the pack had not seen service with one or more of the foxhound or otter hound packs. The type usually measures about eleven to twelve inches at the shoulder and weighs in at about fourteen pounds. Despite my obvious prejudice for the type, good reports of the breed's ratting ability are legion and the type is game, agile and neat with an excellent nose it has inherited from its beagle ancestors. Head type is, at the time of writing at least, a shade variable.

Yet I have seen many whippets which were particularly adept at ratting. Terry Ahern of Tamworth owned an excellent ratting whippet, a frail tiny bitch that showed little enthusiasm for competitive racing, but had a finely developed hunting instinct. This whippet endured fearful rat bites without complaint and also hunted up rats in rubbish with the accuracy of a good terrier. It is a curious fact that some of the very best ratting whippets I have ever seen were track failures, dogs that either refused to run after a dummy hare or dogs which ran indifferently and were obviously aware that the mechanical hare was simply a poor substitute for the real McCoy. It seems as though such dogs have refused to be convinced that their forté lay in chasing clockwork dummies and once they were relieved of their duties on the race track took to conventional hunting with a vengeance.

Such was the case of Lewis Apsey's Pepé who, in the words of one Black Country whippet racer, 'flopped badly on the tracks'. Pepé passed from home to home, because of her reluctance to chase a dummy or a flapping rag, and each new owner, believing he had a racing panacea to liven up the indifferent Pepé, took on the whippet only to find that Pepé simply wouldn't run a clockwork hare. Thus the bewildered Pepé changed hands perhaps a dozen times before she arrived at Lewis' home. At that time Apsey made a living breeding sex-linked poultry mating Rhode Island Red cock birds to light Sussex hens (the result of the union was red/brown hens and silver coloured cock birds). Apsey's farm was not only partly free range but primitive enough to be a haven for rats, and on this farm Pepé came into her own. She spent her days crouched, waiting for rats to leave the sanctuary of the poultry arks and killed them in a trice and her fame was such that word of her spread to South Wales where I lived at the time. By the time I saw her she was a hoary old lady, grey in the muzzle and missing several teeth yet she still caught and killed rats with tremendous panache. It was a pity, but because of her lack of enthusiasm for racing one of her many many owners had the bitch spayed and Pepé never produced progeny.

To return to the subject of terriers which are used for ratting – I always try to break my terriers to ferret while the dogs are still in the nest, or perhaps as soon as the puppies are innoculated would be a more accurate statement. Terrier puppies are often quite fiery and willing to avenge any insult, but their confidence increases as they mature and when fully mature or fully grown they can be very difficult to break to ferrets. Should an inquisitive puppy nose or investigate a ferret a nip from the said ferret will usually stop the puppy in its tracks. Should such a ferret nip an adult terrier the chances are the older terrier will retaliate and ferrets seldom survive the retaliatory bite of a fully grown terrier.

It is possible for ferrets to develop an excellent working relationship with terriers, but only if the terrier learns to treat the ferret with respect. A ferret will often follow out a rat, raging from the conflict with its adversary, and will sometimes strike at any hand or terrier near the burrow. Ferrets can in fact be particularly aggressive with any terrier they find biting a rat with which the ferret has experienced a savage battle. Terriers should be taught to avoid confrontations with ferrets or, if such confrontations occur (and sometimes they are bound to), to back down graciously accepting and forgiving the nip inflicted by an angry ferret. Vampire, one of my own terriers, was a terror with other dogs and a ferocious killer of rats. Yet Vampire would allow a ferret to take outrageous liberties with him. Once when returning from Church Cresly after an extremely abortive rat hunt, a ferret escaped from its box and began to pester the dogs in the trailer in which ferrets and dogs were being carried. If a dog would have threatened Vampire he would have slain it, or else died in the effort, yet when I uncrated the dogs I found Vampire's face pin-pricked with ferret bites and a live unharmed jill in his crate. I reared Vampire, Warlock and Verdelak alongside a litter of ferrets and the trio were used to the caprices of these animals. Had I introduced Vampire to ferrets when he was older I feel matters would have been resolved in a far more bloody fashion. His sister from the litter previous had been reared at a time when distemper had wiped out my ferrets and hence Beltane never grew up with ferrets for she was ten months of age before I considered it safe to reintroduce ferrets to my ferretry. Beltane was never the savage killer Vampire turned out to be but I feel that had she been forced to endure the indignity suffered by Vampire in the trailer she would have bitten and possibly killed the ferret.

As I continued to inbreed to Vampire, his sire and his brother Warlock, my strain became more and more fiery and it became very necessary to break my puppies to ferret before the puppies left the nest. Magog, a pale lemon bitch, not the colour I tried to breed in, was a devil with ferrets when she was a youngster but she outgrew her passion for chasing them and settled down to become a top-grade worker though her children were inclined to be extremely prickly and quick to take offence.

I take young terriers out alone on their first genuine ratting trips and avoid letting them work alongside older terriers simply because I believe individual entering encourages a terrier to use its nose. When two or more terriers are worked together their roles polarise into hunter and catch dog and catch dogs often begin to specialise at their skill so much that they refuse to hunt and mark warrens. Many will simply wait alongside an older, more efficient, hunter and catch the rats as they bolt, but refuse to use their noses to hunt out the presence of rats in rubbish. However should such terriers be started singly, away from the influence exerted by serious hunters or nose dogs, youngsters will start to mark inhabited warrens. Admittedly when such terriers are brought back into the pack situation they assume a role determined by the needs of the rest of the pack – either hunters or catch dogs. However once a puppy has learned to mark and hunt out rats, should seasoned hunters within the pack become *hors de combat* for various reasons the puppy will assume the role of the hunter despite the fact that the whelp is obviously a natural catch dog. Such was the case of Phobos I (I have now another dog called Phobos). Phobos Mark I was started singly marked and hunted up really well before he was returned to the pack in which his mother, Beltane, occupied the role of supreme huntress. Phobos promptly reverted to the role of catch dog and declined to hunt up rats sitting out the fury of the hunt in rubbish and dung piles. He kept this role for three seasons until Beltane whelped another litter and was kept at home on ratting nights. Phobos promptly took over Beltane's role of supreme hunter yet when his dam returned to the pack, Phobos once more reverted to his position as catch dog.

A dog that will mark accurately and well is a great asset to the ferreter who wishes to hunt rat. A great deal of time is saved if a dog can instantly determine if a burrow is inhabited or not. Furthermore ferrets that are encouraged to work uninhabited burrows become decidedly frustrated. Just occasionally certain ferrets will become as reliable as dogs when marking inhabited burrows – though the short life of a ratting ferret ensures the animal must learn the skill quickly or not at all. Rabbiting ferrets, animals of two or three seasons, often become extremely adept at determining whether or not a rabbit is at home. Ratting ferrets will seldom work rats for more than two seasons and hence must learn to mark rat burrows while still kittens. Yet it is bad policy to rely on the marking ability of a ferret if the ferreter has a dog to hand.

A dog that is intended to mark inhabited rat burrows must be left to its own devices to learn the skill, and must never be constantly encouraged to check each and every burrow it encounters. Should the ferreter adopt this very damaging practice the seeds of false marking are so easily sown. Dogs, sensing the pleasure their owner may obtain from seeing the dog mark a burrow, may well begin to mark each and every burrow in the hopes that it will give pleasure to its owner. A marking dog, or rather a dog intended to mark inhabited burrows, should be left to its own devices so that it may determine if the burrow is inhabited or not.

Even mature and sensible dogs can be ruined if their owners persistently encourage a dog to mark at each and every hole. Some years ago I visited Roger Clements of the Hanley Castle kennels with a friend who wished to buy a mature Border terrier bitch that Clements had entered but found not up to standard from the aesthetic point of view. Whatever her failings show-wise she was a superb ratter and from the moment she left the car she checked every heavily scented rat burrow thoroughly and efficiently before giving a positive mark or moving on to another warren. Each time she marked a ferret bolted a rat and my friend seemed highly delighted with his purchase. Weeks later I had cause to hunt with the bitch again and observed that the bitch marked enthusiastically at every hole she encountered whether the holes were inhabited or not.

Quite clearly my friend had encouraged the bitch to 'try' at every burrow and the Border terrier had become a confirmed false marker.

I always encourage a young terrier to work rats that are feeding far from their burrows before taking the youngster on a ferreting foray and most of my best ferreting terriers were seasoned rat catchers before they were allowed to work alongside ferrets. A rat exploding from the confines of a warren moves so rapidly that it invariably escapes the terrier and reaches sanctuary in another burrow. This can be terribly frustrating to a terrier puppy and many terriers seem to lose a little of their edge or enthusiasm when over-matched by ferreted rats. However, should a terrier have experienced some success at rat catching before its first ratting foray then it will be more tolerant of rats that escape it during a ferreting session. Many terriers have become terribly disenchanted before they learn to catch bolting rats and their dismay often becomes very apparent to the ferreter.

Thus only when a terrier has become a proficient rat catcher should it be entered to ferreted rats but, often as not, even the skilled rat catching dog becomes overmatched by its first ferreted rat. The art of ferreting rats – and reader working a terrier to ferreted rats is indeed an art – is to confuse the fleeing rat as much as possible and thereby afford the terrier a chance of catching the rodent. Rats enjoy nesting amongst rubbish and they know the sundry passageways between the bric-a-brac like the backs of their paws. When they decide to bolt before a ferret they know exactly where they are heading and know exactly how to run the route to sanctuary. I find the best way of ensuring a catch is to reconnoitre the spot thoroughly before beginning to ferret, to block off all other burrows and to move pieces of the rubbish across well-established rat runs. This action has a decidedly confusing effect on the rats and because of this confusion the terrier has a fair chance of catching its rats. Quite often the ferret will bolt two or more rats simultaneously and there is every chance that one will be surprised and baffled by the changed landscape it encounters when it bolts. If the terrier is quick and agile it will make good use of this confusion to secure a catch. I find one of the best ways to cover a warren is to kick earth into the hole and then stamp in the earth. Rats will usually run to where the mouth of the burrow was and attempt to dig to safety but if the blocking has been done satisfactorily the rats can be caught by the terrier before rodents dig into the burrow. It is in fact almost a racing certainty that the bolted rat is heading for the safety afforded it by a well worn, well greased rat burrow.

It is wise to make alterations to the landscape adjacent to a burrow as silently as possible. Rats are fairly tolerant about the sound of foot fall above their warrens – they invariably live close to human habitation anyway, but the sound of tumult around the warren may have the effect of preventing them from bolting. The art of ferreting either rats or rabbits is to convince the quarry it is safer to bolt than to face a furious ferret. Hence it is policy to cause the greatest confusion yet to make the least possible noise. I avoid allowing terriers to dig furiously at the mouth of an earth before a ferret is put to ground as, while I do not believe that a rat facing an aggressive ferret will stop to debate the wisdom of bolting, (to bolt or not to bolt perhaps) it is wise not to frighten the rat too much before it meets its Nemesis.

I approach a burrow about to be ferreted with a single dog and ascertain if the lair is still inhabited. Once the dog marks the presence of a rat I remove the dog and then reshuffle the objects adjacent to the burrow scratching in earth into other burrows and pressing in the earth with my boots. When I have judged that the place will be totally confusing to any rat that may decide to bolt, I release the terriers, prevent them snorting into the holes that have been marked by the first dog and allow the dogs to settle before I start ferreting. Only when I have performed the aforementioned tasks do I put a ferret to ground and should the reader be of the opinion that I am too painstaking and that my preparation is a shade too elaborate, I can assure him that my successes repay my efforts ten times over.

At this point a slight digression seems to be in order. From time to time the ferreter may be requested to clear a farmstead or another type of building of its rats. It is absolutely essential to reconnoitre such a spot with a single dog before attempting to ferret the buildings. Should the ferreter arrive at the premises 'cold', so to speak, with terriers and ferrets it is highly likely the owner of the farmstead will show an interest in watching the ferreter at work. On such a foray, unless luck is with the ferreter, it is highly unlikely that a single rat will be caught and the farm owner will be fairly certain to adopt the opinion the ferreter is a complete bungler. Rats may fly everywhere, the sound of terriers may be cacophonous, and in all probability the ferret will kill and lie up to feed on its rat. It is also highly unlikely the ferreter will ever be asked to clear rats from this farmstead ever again for the farm owner is quite correct in his opinion that the ferreter is a crass amateur.

When I was asked to clear an area of rats I visited the area with a single dog, and no ferrets, and asked the owner if I might be allowed to look over the infested property. Few farmsteads are as infested as the owner may declare them to be, for rats have a novel way of making men liars – a single pair of rats out feeding during daylight hours becomes a swarm; a litter of grey rats foraging far from the burrow becomes a plague and an encounter with a single terrified rat after the hours of darkness is related as a scene from a James Herbert novel. A quick check around the farm is now in order for the ferreter to assess how many rats are present and how to catch these rats.

Rat sign is obvious for while rats are furtive, secretive creatures tending to prefer to feed during the hours of darkness they make considerable inroads while feeding. Paths to and from the lairs are usually very well worn and a musky grease smears the mouths of tunnels that are frequently used. Rat droppings shaped like the eggs from Sinbad's roc are scattered at random, but while a rabbit may pass 360 pellets during a day a rat which prefers more concentrated food may pass 15–20 pellets, though more if most of its diet consists of low protein feed such as potatoes. A few rats, a doe with young for instance, will cause a lot of disturbance to the soil near walls when the rats delve into the foundations of buildings. It is also worth noting that a nesting doe may dig several lairs but only seek to nest in one. Hence the presence of a great number of holes does not necessarily indicate the presence of a great number of rats.

Rats live for a short period of time, and a doe of eighteen months of age is considered geriatric, but in the time they are alive they are extremely fecund. Over the years since the brown rat arrived in Britain both naturalists and mathematicians have made reckless stabs at predicting just how many rats could be produced from the issue of a single healthy doe, but few farmsteads are capable of hosting such numbers of rats. The number of rats any area can support is directly related to the food available for those rats and, should the number of rats on a certain farm exceed the ideal number, surplus rats will migrate to other feeding spots. Thus the ratter must always be aware of the fact that he will seldom find really heavy infestations of rats on farmsteads – unless, that is, a farmstead is very badly managed. One of the numerous studies into the ways of brown rats suggests that poisons are seldom efficient at permanently controlling an area of rats, for incoming rats rapidly fill the vacuum left by the poisoned rodents. A far more effective way of controlling rats seems to be to clean up the farmstead and make supplies of food (and water, for rats are thirsty creatures) difficult to obtain. It is in fact possible to make a farm virtually rat proof. The reader must forgive this digression and I will now return to the subject of entering ratting dogs to ferreted rats.

Once a ferret is put to ground dogs should be kept clear of the entrances and exits to rat burrows – but not too clear – and here once again an explanation is essential. Many dogs, particularly dogs that are worked regularly to rat, develop the technique of freezing over the entrance to a rat lair; not moving a muscle and staring into the lair with such intent that the dog is scarcely breathing. Far from deterring rats from bolting the immobility of the dog actually lulls the rat into a false sense of security, so that it bolts into the very jaws of the dog. I have seen a great many very efficient ratting terriers adopt this technique. My veteran dog San, dead this many years, perfected the freezing stance until it was an extremely efficient method of catching ferreted rats. He would allow the rat to crawl completely out of the hole and only when the long ringed tail of the rat left the lair would San snap up his rat. This freezing technique cannot be taught and the dog must acquire it through experience and the terrier must also be allowed to make a great many mistakes to perfect this method of fooling rats into bolting.

Dogs that are held as a ferret works below ground to be slipped only when a rat bolts, are seldom efficient rat catchers. Rats pursued by ferrets explode from the most unlikely spots (they may find an exit from a shallow tunnel simply by scratching through the surface soil) and unless the ferreter is exceptionally vigilant the rat may bolt before the terrier has had an opportunity to notice the slight movement that may preceed the bolting of the rat. Once the terrier is totally steady to the ferret and will desist from placing its muzzle to the holes and snorting down the burrows, a terrier should not be held but allowed to run free. The progress of a subterranean battle between ferret and rat is seldom silent so the terrier is able to follow the progress of the conflict and to be near the mouth of a lair when the rat chooses to bolt. Some terriers become exceedingly adept at following the course of a subterranean battle between rat and ferret. Beltane, one of the foundation bitches of the family, was truly expert at following the way such a battle was progressing. She would move about above a rat run, her head cocked and a look of bewilderment on her face, as out of the corner of her eye she watched the mouth of a lair for the bolting rat. After a while I too could 'read' the progress of the struggle by watching the antics of the bitch and hence I have many 'just ready to bolt' snapshots in my collection of ratting photographs. I bred but two litters from this bitch and this was a pity for she brought many useful genes into the breed.

Throughout the life of my ratting pack I lived in dread of two events, the most terrifying of which was a hunter who insisted on bringing his terrier to a meet; followed closely by the presence of a ratter who insisted on arming himself with a stick while ratting (a stick which, despite my advice and warnings about its use, miraculously appeared if I so much as took my eyes off the hunter).

A maverick terrier, a terrier that insists on running riot and attacking ferrets, is an absolute liability in a team of terriers as is the owner of the said terrier who seems always willing to utter the apocalyptic words 'I'm sure he'll be steady with ferrets' a phrase that is invariably followed by 'I'm astonished that he killed that ferret, I was sure he would be fine with them'. The impact a maverick terrier can make on a perfectly stable sensible group of terriers is alarming to say the least, and once a terrier sees a ferret killed by another dog it will often be unsteady with ferrets for months after the scene it has witnessed. When I first started assembling my rat pack I was beset by strangers with ill-mannered terriers on a leash and requests to come hunting with us. At that time I lacked the panache to be able to disuade hunters from attending our meets with unruly terriers in tow and lacked the moral fibre to stop them. I experienced many accidents, if accidents adequately describes the carnage that took place. Later, at the sight of a strange terrier leaving the visitor's car, I would insist owner and terrier went home regardless of the offence my action caused. It simply was not worth the irritation such an animal and its owner could cause when the terrier rioted on ferret. There are no dogs that are 'may be' steady to ferret. Dogs, particularly terriers, are either broken to ferret, or directly antipathetic to them and these days I am not prepared to take a chance which type of terrier is being brought along to a hunt.

Almost as dangerous as the maverick terrier is the man with a stick: a person who seems to think that a club-sized cudgel is an essential accoutrement for every rat hunt. Such a person is clearly afraid of rats and should he be told to get rid of the cudgel will suddenly find his beloved club as soon as rats start to encircle him. The field master – a somewhat grandiose term for a person who organises a rat hunt – might insist the man throws away his weapon. Indeed the field master may well hide the implement, yet the appearance of the first rat will find the man with a stick, armed and lashing out wildly at the rats around his feet, swearing and behaving badly, despite the fact that prior to the appearance of the rats the same man behaved as impeccably as the organiser of the Lord's Day Observance Society. I have always felt that rats in number have a way of bringing out the very worst in people and my opinion is always reinforced by the appearance of yet another 'man with a stick'.

It is virtually impossible to hit a moving rat with a heavy club, yet the same club is quite lethal to terrier-sized dogs which are almost certain to be hit during the mêlée that follows when rats swarm around the feet of the man with a stick. Before I developed the technique of controlling the field and the courage to send home anyone who showed a tendency to behave wildly many of my terriers were clubbed and not a few badly damaged. After a month or so of repeated accidents I stopped anyone carrying sticks coming on my ratting outings and if a person disregarded the rules – and a few did – they were sent home and never again invited.

A man with a stick of any sort is a liability and must be excluded from any rat hunt where terriers are present.

A man with a stick is a liability, but, for the tops in crass idiocy, it is hard to better a man carrying a gun of any sorts who believes he can hit rats bolting before a ferret but miss terriers. Stunt shooters of this kind should be kept well away from a ferreting session where dogs are involved. The gun carrier too has a characteristic cry 'It'll be all right, don't worry, it'll be all right' and to terminate his song 'Gosh I'm sorry about the dog, I'm really sorry'. The gun carrier must be excluded from any rat hunt where terriers are involved. I have met several of these people, some of whom would leave their guns behind but not before uttering the plaintive bleat 'It'll be all right, I'm sure it'll be all right'. Others have been less cooperative and needed to be sent home and on one occasion I took my pack home rather than chance a dog being shot. The safety of terriers and ferrets should always be of paramount importance during a rat hunt – no matter who it offends!

I always make it a point to ensure my terriers are steady with ferrets and, what is more, stay steady to ferret. When I hunted some four days a week my terriers were in constant contact with ferrets. However once the slack summer season began my terriers were encouraged to drink milk alongside ferrets and brought in contact with them every night when I returned home from school. I never had problems with terriers killing or attacking ferrets as I went out of my way to prevent such attacks. It was often tedious and boring to offer such refresher courses to the terriers, but it paid dividends during the twenty-three years I hunted my pack.

I make no apologies for the extraordinary length of my chapter concerning working ferrets in conjunction with terriers for the very best sport I have experienced has been obtained by ferreting rat and catching them with terriers. At one time I ran a pack of some sixty terriers, the majority of which were bitches in conjunction with ferrets and spent some of the happiest days of my life engaging in such sport. In many ways I suppose I ruined my teaching prospects because of my total preoccupation with ratting, but if I had my life again I don't believe I would live it differently.

Some of my best rat ferreting was obtained at Mexborough, Yorkshire, ferreting rats from the bones and bone ash piles of a maggot factory where rats once abounded. The stench such a place exuded clung to my clothes, my hair, and lingered in my nostrils for days, yet I experienced some incredibly happy times at such a venue.

My diary records a wonderfully good day's hunting on 26 December 1965, a Boxing Day hunt I shared with Keith Foster and the now very famous but then unknown Tony Capstick, the Radio Sheffield disc jockey. My ratting team consisted of some five terriers and four polecat ferrets and during that morning we took an exceptional haul of eighty-nine large adult rats weighing a total of sixty-two pounds. As it was mid-winter the does were neither pregnant nor in the mood for drawing bedding and hence bolted easily before the ferrets. My jills were an excellent team during this time – indeed I wish I had the same team today – and earlier in that year I had purchased them from an allotment holder in the middle of Mexborough. Perhaps the hunts staged at that time were some of the most efficient I have ever organised. My terriers were few enough to be superbly trained, I had an abundance of ferrets (and at that time I used many ferrets during a season's ratting) and despite the curious and apparently effete nature of my ratting com-panions they were a congenial crowd though not particularly dedicated to sporting pursuits. At that time our venue boasted a huge number of rats so the sport was fast and furious and the dogs well entered to rat and completely trustworthy with ferrets. Thus at that period in my life my pack were at their best training-wise and gave the best sport I could imagine. As a minus factor I have to admit that the ratting terriers were at that time very variable (and in the following year or so would become even more variable I should add for beagle blood was creeping into my strain of terrier).

Shortly after this hunt I moved to Lichfield and began breeding terriers in earnest, increasing the proportion of beagle in the mixture and, as a monumental error of judgement, adding bull terrier blood; an action that allowed the hybrids to display glorious heads but caused a spate of fighting the like of which I found intolerable. I lost my ferrets shortly after this cross was made (and many puppies as well) when a new and virulent distemper virus swept the district and I have never man-aged to acquire such game and persistent ratting ferrets since that time, though I had few complaints about the Collingwood-bred greyhound types I should add and I lost much when the old man stopped me using his hobs to maintain the strain (I believe I have already explained the events that led to Collingwood's decision). Be that as it may I never even bred ferrets that had the edge and courage of the kittens I pur-chased in Swinton and Mexborough.

However, it took me a full four years before I obtained a 'ratting pitch' to equal that one I hunted in Yorkshire. I found many poultry farms that yielded a huge crop of rats, but it is inviting trouble, and big trouble at that, to allow ferrets to work poultry farms. A loose ferret, or a ferret that surfaces in an unwanted place, will cause havoc where poultry are con-cerned and once again I must resort to an anecdote to illustrate my point. When I arrived at Lichfield I spent much of my time persuading girlfriends to visit farms to seek out ratting permission and while these requests were usually greeted with a sort of chivalrous amusement by the majority of farm owners, one poultry keeper in Derbyshire reacted in a far from courteous manner. Some young men from Burton-on-Trent had visited the farm just prior to Christmas and requested permission to ferret rat to a mixed bag of lurchers and terriers – a desperately badly organised combination I must add, and one any sane and competent ferreter should avoid. The owner of the farm was plagued by rats that had undermined the turkey pens and eaten young table ducklings alive (an extremely grisly sight I must add) and hence he was unwise enough to welcome the youths to his farm. Now personally the sight of lurchers running with terriers sets my teeth on edge for it is symptomatic of a chaotic day's hunting by any standards. However to return to the tale. The poultry farmer apparently displayed a remarkable tolerance to the fact that one of the lurchers attempted to haul ducks through the wires, and was remarkably forgiving about the fact the terriers chopped and killed a hen that had escaped from the poultry houses. He was however a shade less forgiving when a ferret surfaced in the turkey pen and caused the crazed birds to pile atop of each other suffocating the bottom-most layer of turkeys. This action triggered off the terriers and the lurchers that promptly seized the wings and legs that protruded through the wire netting of the pens and proceeded to haul the wretched birds piecemeal through the wires. I am not quite sure as to whether insurance companies are required to recompense any farmer for such chaos reminiscent of a bloodier version of Gerard Hoffnung's *Man and the Barrel* soliloquy, but whatever the financial outcome of the mishap the poultry keeper left us in no doubt about his feelings about ferrets and terriers. Needless to say he did not give us permission to ferret his smallholding.

In time I acquired large amounts of ferreting permission on pig farms and the reputation my dogs had for being steady with stock soon brought us more ferreting permission than I could possibly manage. Hence the night hunting trips for which my pack later became famous began and of course on such ventures it was impossible or unwise to use ferrets. The pig boom ceased abruptly in 1969 and most wise pig farmers sold out the following year leaving my pack only poultry houses to work, though by this time we were able to ferret two small maggot factories and a host of rather unsavoury smallholdings that existed just beyond the reach of the Public Health officials.

By this time my pack numbered some twenty-five terriers and the boost given me by the acquisition of the last of the Collingwood greyhound ferrets served me extremely well (and it is a tragedy I did not have the foresight to continue the strain in its pure form).

However to have twenty well-trained and stock-broken ferreting terriers is no mean feat and to keep such a team in line is difficult in the extreme. It was however even more difficult to prevent visitors to the hunts, sometimes uninvited visitors one should add, from bringing terriers to our meets and these unbroken terriers caused havoc when they were presented with the sight of droves of bolted rats followed by somewhat slower, and hence more vulnerable, ferrets. By this time an invitation to the meets had become prestigious and it was necessary to exclude uninvited outsiders completely, and the 'field' was limited to twelve regulars who worked with the pack as much as they observed the hunt.

Despite the trials and tribulations of running a rat pack – and the problems I encountered were often terrifying, should I have a chance to relive my life I would not have missed one minute of the rat hunts. Whyte Melville is often quoted as saying 'The best of my pleasure has been with horse and hound'. My most happy times were experienced with terriers and ferrets.

13

Ferret Shows

On 8 April 1967, Wilf Deakin, a gamekeeper whose name regularly appeared in the 'Letters to the Editor' column of various sporting papers 'phoned me to request that I judged a ferret show. At first I thought Wilf was playing a trick on me, revenge perhaps for a hideous practical joke that occurred at Bill Brockley's farm in the January of that year. However after a few moments I realised Wilf was deadly serious. At that time Brockley was winning at these shows, and Wilf wanted a side event to attract a bigger gate and produce greater enthusiasm for attending country shows.

However, to cut quite a lengthy story short, I declined Wilf's offer to judge what was possibly the first show that catered exclusively for ferrets and I believe Wilf later abandoned the idea of staging the exhibition. My reasons for refusing or declining to judge this show were legion. Firstly, at that time at least the idea would have seemed mildly ridiculous, or at the very least quaint, and rather silly. Secondly, I did not feel I was qualified to judge such a show – though to nominate anyone who was qualified would have been quite a task! True, I had kept ferrets for many years and I had outgrown the notion that I had nothing to learn about livestock – and it is essential that any judge of any sort dispenses with the notion he is omniscient post haste. Lastly, I had handled far too many ferrets that were slightly maladjusted. Thus I was reluctant to chance my hands examining, assessing and perhaps judging ferrets that were hell bent on eating my hands and fingers – and eating them in public I should add – the ultimate humiliation. Hence I declined, not graciously perhaps but very decisively, and henceforth I was never again asked to judge a ferret show.

These days ferret shows are part and parcel of every country fair and there are specialist ferret clubs such as G.E.M. that stage ferret exhibitions quite independently of other country shows. There are also, so I am reliably informed, ferret judges who are both competent and give the

Ferret shows are popular and the prizes for winners often spectacular

appropriate histrionic displays while assessing the merits, virtues and faults of ferrets. These shows are invariably well run, free of the bizarre incidents that mar lurcher shows and make what should be a pleasant day out an embarrassing nightmare.

Personally I endorse the idea of ferret shows or anything that improves the lot of the common or garden ferret, for many ferrets get a very raw deal from their owners. Contrary to the popular belief, any ferret that is brushed, cleaned and presented in a glowing healthy condition can also be worked extremely hard. In fact a ferret in good condition will give a better account of itself at rat or at rabbit than will a half-starved brute kept in a damp hutch and fed a slop diet. What is more important is the fact that many ferret clubs often plough back whatever funds are made at these shows into ferret welfare – the investigation of diseases and the production of vasectomised hobs – a boon to stop the overbreeding of ferrets that sees hundreds of surplus kittens produced each summer – and sold for a song often to unsuitable people.

It would be difficult to imagine a more fairly judged event than a ferret show. Ferrets are usually boxed prior to the show and each box given a number with no indication of who actually owns the ferret. Judges must then determine which ferret is the most superior animal both in condition and conformation regardless of the anonymous owner of the animal. Hence comments such as 'he's judging the wrong side of the leash' (or its musteline equivalent) can never be applied to the ferret judge – particularly as it is very difficult to tell one white ferret from another, even though fitch or polecat ferrets often have distinctive facial patterns.

Clearly the good condition of the stock should be of paramount importance to the ferret judge. A clean healthy ferret should be lean but not emaciated with clean vermin-free fur and sound feet, free from the foot ailments (once very common amongst ferrets) that bespeak that ferrets are kept in damp hutches with urine stained floors. A healthy ferret has a clean, albeit musky, scent, a scent that also bespeaks the conditions under which the ferret is kept. Unless the show is a 'one horse affair' a dirty ferret, one shown in messy condition, has little chance of winning at a ferret show particularly as ferrets are undemanding creatures which require little luxury to keep them clean and healthy. I am notoriously remiss about regularly cleaning out my ferrets yet my stock is always clean and healthy. Thus a dirty unkempt looking ferret has clearly been kept in some extremely unpleasant conditions.

However after a season's rabbiting, or worse still a season's ratting, a ferret is quite likely to have unwanted guests residing in its coat. Thus some two weeks before a show it is wise to dust both the ferret and its nesting compartment bedding with a non-toxic insecticide and it is

Well handled ferrets are safe with young children

good sense to investigate whether a proprietary brand of insecticide is injurious to ferrets – and some insecticides can kill ferrets. Few ferrets need to be bathed prior to a show, though many exhibitors employ this technique of cleaning a ferret. Some ferrets are so clean and deodorised that they no longer have the faint musky odour that is characteristic of a healthy ferret.

As to the conformation of a ferret, many ferret judges have very different ideas as to what constitutes an ideal shape. At the time of writing very tiny weasel-like ferrets are popular with judges, though such ferrets often suffer quite badly when subjected to a hard day's rabbiting and tiny ferrets are hopelessly overmatched by a large and furious doe rat. Likewise very big hobs seem to be unpopular with ferret judges though such hobs certainly have their uses as line ferrets – and I have seen some enormous ferrets that were satisfactory liners.

Medium-sized hobs seem to win well at ferret shows and frankly medium-sized jills would be my choice as well. Ferrets should be judged as to their suitability to work rabbit or rat and such peculiarities as to the shape, head size and head shape should be of secondary importance to the ferret judge. Personally I should select my winners from the medium-sized ferrets after I had cast out very tiny jills or huge outsized hobs.

Long slinky ferrets of the type once known as greyhound ferrets are much prized by show judges and fat, large bellied, short stumpy animals, no matter how efficient these animals may be at their work, are not popular at ferret shows. Furthermore ferrets with long thin finely sculpted heads are popular with most judges. In fact early ferreting books penned during the nineteenth century advise the ferreter to choose only ferrets with stoat-like heads, despite the fact that a strong powerful short muzzle is obviously better for handling a foe with the disposition of a rat. Nevertheless ferrets with short powerful muzzles are seldom as eye catching as dolichocephalic (narrow-headed) ferrets.

There are usually several classes for show/exhibition/benched ferrets except, of course, in small shows where few ferrets are exhibited. Classes are usually staged according to colour, sex and age for example:

White hob adult
White jill adult
White jill kitten
White hob kitten
Polecat / sandy kitten hob
Polecat / sandy kitten jill
Polecat / sandy adult hob
Polecat / sandy adult jill
Best kitten
Best adult

In recent years a new class has appeared on certain show schedules; namely 'any other colour' and certainly unusually coloured ferrets have appeared in recent years. Black-eyed white ferrets, identical in shade to albino ferrets but without the red eyes that are typical of true albino ferrets, are now common. More unusual still are ferrets that are almost identical to tourmaline sapphire-coloured mink. These strange, beautiful and exotic coloured ferrets are not a whit inferior as workers because of their peculiar hues. At the first meeting of the N.L. and R.C. working lurcher trials at Blaengarw in 1991 a tourmaline-coloured ferret worked unfailingly throughout the day in such a manner that it put most of my own conventionally coloured white ferrets to shame.

Ferret shows should be treated as fun, a day out for the family so to speak. If such shows are treated as serious events, events that are imperative for the exhibitor to win, a great deal will be lost. Ferret shows are however quite important simply because they encourage ferret welfare societies to be formed and a spin off from such societies is a better education concerning the needs and working of ferrets.

Perhaps I was wrong in refusing Wilf Deakin's offer to judge ferrets.

14

Diseases of the Ferret

When I first penned *Modern Ferreting* in 1976 there was little known about the sundry malaises that afflicted the ferret. Mange, a common affliction of ferrets that were used to hunt rat, was treated with powdered sulphur mixed into molten vaseline, and curiously this remedy was sometimes successful in treating the infection. Foot rot or mange of the feet was often treated with a poisonous copper sulphate solution or Mycota ointment. Deep wounds were cleaned and an antibiotic cream applied to the wound and, if the ferreter was lucky, the vet would prescribe an antibiotic other than penicillin for a few years later it was realised that ferrets were allergic to penicillin and penicillin-related antibiotics. If the vet was unfortunate enough to prescribe penicillin the ferret often died (though some admittedly recovered) and the ferreter went out and bought another ferret. Ferrets have always been cheap, ridiculously cheap in fact, and it was invariably cheaper to buy another ferret than pay to have a sick ferret treated. If the ferreter valued the animal enough to have it treated the chances were that the veterinary surgeon who would never have treated a ferret before, would have reached for that universal specific the antibiotic and should that anti-biotic be penicillin-related – well, ferrets were always cheap to replace anyway. Hence my chapter concerning ferret diseases is a collection of homespun remedies, some of which worked and some of which – well, ferrets were easy to replace weren't they?

However, in 1987 I received a letter from a veterinary surgeon, J.H. Lewington of Craigie, Western Australia, requesting that he quoted my inheritance table from *Modern Ferreting*, for Lewington was compiling a 'ferret compendium' for the T.G. Hungerford Vade Meium Series for Domestic Animals. Lewington's work is hardly essential reading for the hunter. Indeed it makes scant reference to the techniques of rabbit hunting and merely mentions that ferrets can be used to hunt rat. What the Hungerford booklet has however is an elaborate and well-researched chapter on the diseases that trouble the ferret and for this reason alone the book makes essential reading for the ferreter who cares for his stock.

Prior to Lewington's monograph there had been little serious research conducted concerning the pathology of the ferret, for ferrets, unlike mink, had little economic value. Admittedly some investigation into the gross anatomy of ferrets had been conducted by German anatomists when fitch farming (rearing polecat ferrets in order to secure their lustrous furs) enjoyed a temporary financial boom. Furthermore, when ferrets began to be used as laboratory animals that were used to test human influenza vaccines interest in ferret welfare was rekindled. However, the ferret keeper would fare rather less than well exploring the highly complex scientific papers concerning ferret pathology and rely on the excellent booklet by Lewington as a guide to ferret welfare. I would also advise that ferret keepers seeking veterinary assistance for their wards should supply their veterinary surgeon with the Hungerford monograph, for most vets have precious little knowledge of how to cure the diseases that plague ferrets.

Might I retract the expression 'diseases that plague ferrets' immediately, for ferrets kept dry, moderately clean and fed on a flesh diet are seldom ill or even below par condition-wise. Once again I confess I am notoriously slovenly about cleaning out my ferrets, or checking on their welfare in mid-winter for I leave on my daily ferreting forays before dawn picking out the first ferrets that clamber up the bars of the cage returning them home and feeding and watering them after dark. They are cleaned out when I remember to do so for my ferret cage is truly gigantic and well-designed by Curtis Price of Newton. Yet despite the apparently cavalier way in which I treat my ferrets, illness among them is rare and frankly, practically non-existent yet my dogs regularly sniff at the ferret cage and lick the bars to savour the musky odour all ferrets, male and female alike, seem to emit. Yet if ferrets are kept dry, furnished with deep bedding to allow them to stay warm, fed a nutritious diet and given sufficient exercise to keep them lean and active it is unusual to find an ailing ferret.

Yet working ferrets are liable to become infected with numerous endo-parasites and Lewington offers an interesting tale of what he calls stickfast fleas, or fleas that often cover the ears of Australian rabbits that have become infected with myxomatosis. Jills infested with fleas of this variety will often lose their litters when the kittens are four to six weeks old. Lewington also records that he has observed a young, weaned ferret kitten die from a severe infestation of fleas (he does not state which kind of fleas though ferrets can host poultry, cat and rabbit fleas as well as the pernicious Australian stickfast fleas Echidophaga Mymecobil).

Yet it is relatively easy to cleanse the ferret of any of these fleas. Pet shampoos, the mildest of pet shampoos one must add, will usually rid the ferret of any of the above mentioned fleas, and rid the animal of tics and lice to boot. Ratting ferrets are particularly prone to flea infestations, particularly ferrets that kill and lie up on the body of a rat for a night or so. Fleas leave the cooling body of a rat and seek sanctuary on the warm body of the killer. At one time my ratting ferrets were kept clear of parasites by regularly (once every two weeks) dipping them in an insecticidal shampoo I made up from a sheep dip and washing up liquid.

Lewington advises a pyrethrum-based shampoo called *Pet Gloss* shampoo, readily available in Australia but seldom seen in British pet shops, but pyrethrum-based pet shampoos are becoming very common in Europe and are replacing gamma benzene hexachloride based products.

However, the curse of the ratting ferret is mange and the rat hunter would do well to watch out for signs of this particularly unpleasant skin infection. Mange will usually appear on the extremities of the ferret's body denuding the face, ears, feet and tail of fur and causing the ferret to scratch madly. Lewington attributes the once common foot rot to the effects of the sarcoptic mite, but in all probability what is referred to as foot rot in Australia is not related to the foot rot that was once the bane of British ferrets kept in wet cages.

Sarcoptic mange is easily cleaned if the ferret keeper is vigilant. Wooden cages that can host the parasite in the nooks and crannies of the woodwork are best cleaned with a blow lamp and the bedding in which the ferret is housed should be burned. It is in fact rather ludicrous to carefully treat the ferret for mange and yet allow the ferret to return to an uncleaned cage. Sarcoptic mange mites are still extremely susceptible to sulphur ointments. Old-fashioned remedies such as ointments made by adding flowers of sulphur to lard or other animal fats are still quite successful. I cannot resist mentioning the panacea used by Collingwood who made up a hell brew that was dark brown in colour and stank of ammonia. Collingwood would treat any ferret brought to him with this pungent slime which he assured me was efficacious at curing fleas, lice, tics and mange. What Collingwood used to make up this mixture will probably never be known yet he claimed Youngs of Misterton, who also sold mange remedies, would have paid him to sell them his secrets. It was not uncommon to see Collingwood's ferrets daubed in this brown grease, yet I never saw an infected animal in Collingwood's ramshackle ferretry. I spoke to Marian, Collingwood's only daughter, shortly after her father's death but she showed little interest in her father's nostrums except to say that as a young man her father had worked on the railways and engine grease was the basis of most of his homespun cures.

Lewington too advises sulphur based mangicides – lime, sulphur sprays and shampoos in which the ferret should be immersed and kept in the solution for at least five minutes after which the sulphur wash should be allowed to dry on the ferret's fur. Lewington advises that this treatment should be repeated every four weeks until the infection is clear.

It is worth noting that sarcoptic mange is highly contagious and can be transmitted to human beings where it produces a disease known as scabies – a maddeningly itching disease that can easily convince the ferret keeper of the unfortunate lot of a ferret infected with this malaise. I cannot resist a tale concerning scabies, so perhaps the reader will bear with me for a few lines. Despite the fact that I am relatively clean and bathe fairly (if not very) frequently, I am notoriously susceptible to scabies. When I taught in inner city areas where scabies and lice were all too common, I frequently became infected with scabies until, that is, I discovered (and this sounds a shade like a television commercial) the merits of Bob Martin's dog shampoo or insecticidal dog soap. From the time I first started using these products, until I left the teaching profession, I was never infected with either scabies or lice. In 1973 my ferreting team worked a particularly nasty pig farm to clear it of rats. My ferrets promptly became very mangy as did my dogs – and my fellow ferreters. Only one of the group escaped the ravages of mange and scabies and for this I have to thank the Bob Martin's dog shampoo and soaps. Actually, absurd as the tale may sound, it is good policy for anyone who works ferrets to rats to bathe using an insecticidal soap such as Derbac rather than products specifically designed to cater for the needs of dogs.

Ferrets that are worked to rabbits in areas where foxes are common (and foxes will lie up in rabbit burrows) are prone to what is called ear mange or ear canker. Ferrets afflicted with these mites can become very distressed and will shake their heads as though demented and rub their heads on the wires of their cages. Yet this infection too can be treated, though the ferreter should always be observant about the ways his wards behave and if possible treat the infections as soon as symptoms are observed. Any ear canker cure will clear up the infection in a matter of days though it is good stockmanship to continue to treat the infected ferrets for some weeks after the infection has apparently cleared.

When ferrets are worked in conjunction with dogs it is wise to vaccinate the ferrets against distemper. The incubation period for this disease is roughly seven days, after which the ferret loses weight, attempts to vomit and scours badly. A red rash often appears along the jawline of the ferret and the bare belly of the ferret assumes a dappled red appearance. In some cases the ferret's feet swell and the pads become hardened (compare this to hard pad, a form of distemper that attacks dogs). Once the ferret displays these symptoms death invariably follows the infection within fourteen to sixteen days and there is virtually no treatment for this disease. I have yet to see an uninnoculated ferret survive an attack of distemper and Lewington too describes the infection as one hundred per cent fatal. I now innoculate all my ferrets against this disease – I split a canine distemper vaccine ampule some five ways to bring about this innoculation programme, but prior to the time I innoculated my ferrets I lost some of the best ratting ferrets I have ever owned to the ravages of canine distemper. Sadly, though my innoculation programme has been entirely successful, I have never been able to breed such quality ratting ferrets again. It is also worth stating that since that time I have observed several distemper outbreaks in the district where I lived but have never observed an innoculated ferret die or take ill when distemper visited my ferretry.

It must seem extremely strange to the tyro ferret keeper but it is a fact that ferrets are notoriously susceptible to human influenza or, to be more precise, forms of human influenza. Yet laboratory bred ferrets are regularly used to test certain influenza vaccines. Influenza itself seldom kills a ferret but the disease can, if not treated, reduce the ferrets resistance to other infections to such a state that the ferret may well develop pneumonia. Lewington states that the disease has an incubation period of some forty- eight hours after which the ferret refuses to eat and experiences a slight rise in temperature (a ferret's body temperature is normally 40°C or 104°F) and the ferret is subject to bouts of sneezing – though many irritants, including straw dust or the use of certain disinfectants, may well cause similar bouts of sneezing.

Lewington advises giving the ferret a course of broad spectrum antibiotics (not penicillin one should add) and keeping the animal warm. Ferrets apparently recover from the infection in a matter of five or so days and achieve immunity to the particular strain of influenza virus for five or so weeks. It is interesting to note that in 1964 ferrets fell ill some two weeks after their handlers experienced the symptoms of influenza.

Whether or not ferrets are susceptible to leptospiral jaundice, or rat catchers yellows, is a moot point though Lewington believes that while the disease is rare in Australia ferrets may contract the disease. Yet for some thirty years I regularly fed my ferrets on the cadavers of rats and despite the fact that Monlux 1964 showed that in a sample of one hundred rats fifty-five had leptospirosis in their kidneys I have never known a ferret show any of the symptoms of this ailment – though innoculated dogs frequently died in places where I caught the rats to feed my ferrets.

However one of the most terrifying diseases that has started to infect ferrets in recent years is Aleutianism or Aleutians disease. This disease was noticed in captive mink reared in the USA and the virus isolated in 1956. Mink infected with this virus fail to thrive, lose weight rapidly, develop an abnormal thirst and pass undigested food in their faeces. Later, the infected animals may bleed from the mouth and become anaemic whereupon death follows within a month of the onset of the infection. At one time only the dark grey Aleutian mink were considered susceptible to the disease (hence the name Aleutianism) but other varieties of mink also began to die from the disease in later years.

When the disease began to infect ferrets is debateable, and how ferrets first contracted the disease is a mystery. Two theories have been postulated. Firstly the disease may have always existed in ferrets and wild polecats but it is only in recent years that ferrets have become particularly susceptible to the virus. Now curiously in the 1950s Haagerdoorn, the now quite discredited Dutch geneticist, stated that he believed that a wild stock of animals and plants should be kept at hand in order that when the cultivated varieties of these plants or animals become less resistant to disease an outcross to the wild species would give a genetic shot in the arm so to speak. Few scientific researchers paid heed to Haagerdoorn's notions – and the term notion rather than hypothesis best described his highly unscientific reasoning, yet perhaps Haagerdoorn did stumble on some scientific truth.

Yet another theory is that the nature of the virus has changed slightly and begun to infect ferrets for the symptoms manifested by infected ferrets are virtually identical to those displayed by infected mink – and this must seem a fairly logical hypothesis for not only are the species of mustelid closely related but sometimes fall victim to the same diseases – distemper etc.

I feel something of a fraud writing about Aleutian's disease for while I have observed the havoc the ailment caused in commercial mink farms I have yet to encounter the disease amongst ferrets. Yet may I once more advance one of the heretical hypotheses for which I am fairly notorious. Is it possible that Aleutians disease, or its ferreting equivalent, has always existed amongst ferrets. Far too many ferrets die of causes unknown and the cadavers of these ferrets are seldom subjected to systematic autopsies. Ferrets are so easily obtained and, what is worse, so cheaply obtained, that ferret keepers simply bury their dead ferrets and seek out new stock to replace the dead animals – 'it died of some'at', seems to be the elegy uttered by most ferret keepers.

Yet the disease is a dangerous one. Mink farmers lived in dread of an outbreak of the ailment, and at one time once a single animal was diagnosed as suffering from the disease the whole mink farm was cleared of stock and the premises cleansed with bleach and left fallow for several months before restocking with mink again. Lewington advises innoculation of all mink but no suitable vaccine exists to protect ferrets from the ravages of this infection.

Ferrets will apparently survive an attack of Aleutians disease, though apparently even after the ferret has recovered from this disease it can be infectious for a further six to nine months and the disease carried from a carrier to a healthy ferret by human agencies.

Diagnosis is only possible if a sample of the ferrets blood is obtained by clipping a toenail to the quick, extracting a sample of blood from the bleeding quick and subjecting the blood sample to a process known as C.I.P. an abbreviation for counter immunecletro phoresis.

Apparently the disease has only been reported in Wessex but the reader would be wise to consider the hypothesis I advanced earlier – namely the ferret has always been a victim of unknown diseases and according to Stephen W. Cooke, in February 1992 one in eight ferrets in Britain may be suffering from Aleutians disease.

Whether or not veterinary science will find it sufficiently financially worthwhile to devise a vaccine to protect the ferret from Aleutians disease is questionable – the ferret, despite its many uses and often endearing character, is so easily obtained and alas so inexpensive to replace that it is scarcely worthwhile to treat a ferret for any disease.

Bibliography

The following books might be of interest to ferreters

Ferreting and Trapping for Amateur Gamekeepers, Guy Smith
   Quite an interesting book published in 1978 and now just a shade dated.

Rabbits and their History, John Sheail
   A must for anyone who is interested in the conquering march of the rabbit and also an easy read.

Pugs and Drummers, John Marchington
   This is a delightful book and one I have read many times. Marchington deals with the predator/prey relationship of the rabbit/ferret in a very easy to read manner and I am surprised this book is not more readily available. Faber and Faber should consider republishing this epic.

The Complete Book of Ferrets, Val Porter and Nicholas Brown
   A nicely presented, well-written book – one that is indeed a hard act to follow. Essential reading for those who keep ferrets as pets as well as for hunters.

The Ferret and Ferreting Handbook, James McKay
   A well-produced book that achieves the correct balance between hard factual data and anecdote. This book too deals with the ferret as a pet as well as a hunting companion.

The Ferret and Ferreting Guide, Graham Welstead
   A well-illustrated attractive book with excellent illustrations. It was published in 1981 and is still available.

Ferrets and Ferreting, Peter Whitaker
   A fine little booklet by a man who is a dedicated rabbit hunter.

The Shooting Times Guide to Ferreting, Fred J. Taylor
   This is a fine book written as only Fred can write. For those who have enjoyed Fred's articles in *Shooting Times* this is a welcome addition to Taylor literature. I enjoyed this book greatly and envy Fred's style of writing.

Useful Addresses

Ferret Clubs

N.F.W.S.
   Mrs K. Lathaen, Meadow View, Pheasants Hill, Hambleden, Henley-on-Thames, Oxfordshire RG9 6SN

Gloucester Ferreters
   c/o J. Petchey, 16 Finchcroft Lane, Prestbury, Glos. GL52 5BG

Sussex F.W.S.
   Duncan McArthur, 18 The Slides, St Leonards on Sea, Hastings, TN38 9LE

Essex F.W.S.
   Wendy Smith, 21 Moreton Road, Shelley, Ongar, Essex CM5 0AP

Kent Ferreters
   Kevin Walker, 21 Southwell Road, Strood, ME2 2RS

S.E. Ferrets
   Ray Boorman, Westbury, 2 Warren Street, Lenham, Kent

Coventry and Warks. Ferrets
   Eric Holmes, 18 Links Road, Radford, Coventry, CV6 23DN

Wessex Ferret Club
   Tom Sturgess, 9 The Retreat, Hounsdown, Totton, Hampshire SO4 4FW

STIF VAST
   Per-Erik Jorgensen, Norra Barnsjiov 19, 437 35 Lindome, Sweden

Fretchen Club Berlin
   Karin Schneider, Fuchsienweg 18A, D-1000 Berlin 47, Germany

Swiss Ferret Club
   Urs Murbach, Hardstrasse 41, 5432 Neuenhof, Switzerland

Stichting De Fret
   Nel Smeding, Ariana Nozemanstraat 15hs, 1065 TP Amsterdam, The Netherlands

5th Australia Ferret Assocn.
   C/O 6 Howard Street, Windsor Gardens, S.A. 587

Welfare Societies

Kent Ferret Welfare Society
 0233 624688. John Hopkin, 5 Eastern Gardens, Willesborough, Ashford
 Kent TN24 0HE

Hertfordshire Ferret Welfare Society
 Pat Tyler, 138 Turners Hill, Hemel Hempstead, Hertfordshire HP2 4LW

Cambridgeshire Ferret Welfare and Rescue Society
 Amanda Wood, 37 Payne Avenue, Wisbech, Cambridgeshire, PE13
 3HS

London Ferret Rescue Centre
 071 733 8631 (24 hour rescue). Mr S. Dooley, 4 Gauden Road,
 Clapham, London SW4